Lessons From the Light

A True Story of Angels and Healing

Myra Starr *with* **John Mulkey**

WisdomWorks Press
P.O. Box 904
Waleska GA 30183

ISBN: 0985935308
ISBN 13: 9780985935306

Disclaimer

This book is a true account of one person's experiences and is not intended as a substitute for medical advice or treatment. Individual health concerns should always be discussed with a qualified medical practitioner. The authors and publisher disclaim any liability arising directly or indirectly from the reading, interpretation, or use of this book.

Cover design by: R. Scott Lewis

Dedication

This book is dedicated to all those Healers, Angels, and Masters who surround us each day with their loving energy and who are ready to offer their guidance whenever we ask and listen.

TABLE OF CONTENTS

Prologue

Once or twice in a lifetime we experience events that are hardly noticeable when they occur, but in retrospect are recognized as having great significance, often changing the direction of our lives. My first encounter with Myra Starr was just such an event.

We met in the fall of 1994. Myra was living in Dahlonega, Georgia, a small town at the foot of the Appalachian Mountains. Though I had no idea at the time, our meeting was both powerful and synchronistic. For me, it marked the beginning of a profound change in a life that had struggled for decades to discover its purpose. With her help I reconnected with my true self, a part that had remained hidden for years.

In late October, while attending a wedding, I was approached by a long-time friend, Jean. She told me the most incredible story. A friend of hers, suffering from cancer, had recently been treated by a Native American healer named Myra Starr, and had apparently experienced a miraculous improvement. Jean's background as a nurse gave credence to her story. As she told me of her friend's experiences, I wanted to know more. She suggested I consider taking my granddaughter, Lindsay, to see the healer.

A victim of cystic fibrosis, Lindsay had suffered the debilitating effects of the disease for most of her seven years, regularly requiring hospitalization. I was desperate for a miracle and willing to try anything, regardless of how unorthodox it might seem.

I had spent years searching for some way to help her, examining more alternative healing methods than I had previously known to have existed. I worked with healers in this country, and studied with some from as far away as China and the Philippines. They willingly shared their knowledge of plants, herbs, and the human energy field, but nothing I learned seemed to make much difference. The techniques I used with Lindsay brought little more than short-term relief, not the dramatic reversal of her disease I sought; but I refused to give up. If Jean's friend had been helped, perhaps the healer could help Lindsay. I prayed she could. I wondered if Myra Starr held the key I'd been seeking.

Jean told me that Myra had recently been taped for an upcoming segment of an NBC special about angels and healing. The show would air within a couple of weeks. Certain that the TV appearance would dramatically increase the number of people wanting to see her, I felt it urgent to contact her as soon as possible.

I called the number Jean had given me, and a female voice answered. "Are you Myra," I asked, "the one who does healing?"

"Yes. How can I help you?"

I'm not sure what I expected—her to instinctively know what I wanted or for me to have some sense I had reached someone with supernatural abilities—but neither happened. I paused for a moment hoping I was making the right choice.

I explained who I was and began to tell her about Lindsay. She listened without interruption. When I finished, I asked if she thought she could help. Her answer was hardly comforting. She wouldn't predict what the results would be. I was skeptical, but desperate, wondering if she was just another charlatan, bilking the sick and helpless. However, her response offered encouragement when she announced, "Of course, there will be no charge. The good I accomplish comes from Spirit. I'm only a channel through which healing may occur." Her subsequent questions seemed to demonstrate genuine concern for my ailing granddaughter.

I scheduled a time for Lindsay to meet with Myra and spent the next few days trying to learn as much as I could about her. The information was sketchy, a magazine article and a few anecdotes about her recent healing experiences—the most notable of which had occurred during the taping of the NBC special, *Angels II, Beyond the Light.*

The lady suffering from cancer and had also been in search of a miracle. She had agreed to participate, allowing herself to be filmed as the healer worked with her. And, to the surprise of everyone, including her physician, her strength had increased substantially, and the pain that had plagued her for months had practically disappeared. Her doctor, who agreed to be interviewed for the show, confirmed that his patient had experienced a remarkable and inexplicable improvement. Though he stopped short of giving credit to the healer, his obvious bewilderment over what had caused the change gave me reasons for hope.

On the day of our visit, I talked with Lindsay as we drove into the Georgia mountains. I tried to comfort her and to allay her fears about the treatment to come, aware that during her brief life she had already experienced more doctor visits than most do in a lifetime.

"Don't worry," I told her, "this lady won't hurt you. She just wants to see if she can make you feel better. This will be fun."

Following the directions the healer had provided, we were soon winding along a gravel lane into a campground. My level of confidence began to shrink. The place was a county park, filled with small travel trailers and motor homes. I maneuvered down the narrow drive, stopping in front of the office. I had hardly stepped from the car when the healer appeared from the office door.

"You must be John." She extended her hand. "I'm Myra." I gazed at the figure before me. She was dressed in an outfit that seemed from another time—buckskins, moccasins, and a wide woven belt with a large silver buckle. Leather pouches and other objects swung from the belt; and her long graying hair almost reached her waist.

After I introduced her to Lindsay, we were led to a small building that appeared to be nothing more than a converted storage shed. "This is my healing room," she said. She motioned us inside.

The walls were covered with Native American symbols and pictures. A massage table stood in the center of the room. After helping Lindsay onto the table, she had her lie down, covering her with a brightly colored Indian blanket.

Myra talked to us about what she would do. "I'll be using some stones," she said, "and I may place them on your body." She squeezed Lindsay's hand. "Don't worry. I won't do anything to hurt you. I may sing you a song, and I might even smoke my pipe." The healer's broad smile and reassuring tone seemed to rid my granddaughter of her fears, and she grew calm. I was more relaxed too, comforted by Myra's simple demeanor and soothing voice.

She spent the next thirty minutes or so moving her hands back and forth around Lindsay's slender body, occasionally pausing to place small stones on or beside her. As she worked she sang a haunting and beautiful melody, the words of which seemed from another language. I watched and prayed, hoping for a miracle.

When she had finished, Myra talked with us for several minutes and made a few suggestions for things Lindsay should eat. She circled her arms around my granddaughter and held her close as if by sheer strength she could draw the disease from her body.

During the entire process Lindsay appeared more comfortable than I had seen her in months. And from that day forward there were remarkable improvements in some of her symptoms.

We returned to see Myra on several occasions. Lindsay seemed aware that Myra was helping her and looked forward to the visits. Sadly, although her visits with Myra did make the disease less painful for her, Lindsay died two years after our first visit.

Months later I would learn that the last time we had visited the healer, she had sensed death was near. Myra would later tell me that when we pulled into her drive, she had been unable to see my granddaughter sitting next to me in the car. Lindsay's energy body had grown so weak that it was practically invisible. Without touching her, Myra's knew it was time, but she also knew she couldn't share her vision with me.

A few weeks after that final visit, Lindsay died. At the time it was impossible for me to let her go. We had been the best of friends, and I had made it my mission to save her life. The nine years we had shared were simply not enough. She had trusted me to help her, and I had failed.

I sobbed as I gave Myra the news. "I know you wanted to heal her," she said. "We all did. But some of the things that happen to us in this life are beyond our ability to understand. You gave her the best part of you. You loved her.

During the months we visited Myra, I had developed both a respect for the healer's dedication and a bond that survived my wishes for my granddaughter. I was drawn to her wisdom, her healing abilities, and her compassion. Though I no longer needed her powers for Lindsay, we had become friends, connected by our mutual interest in healing, and I occasionally visited with her as I struggled through my grief.

Although Myra was unaware—at least I had not told her—I was also in a period of transition, having abandoned a twenty-five year career as a construction executive to pursue my long-time ambition to become a writer. My experiences with Lindsay had intensified my interest in alternative healing, and I wanted to write about what I had learned. I began working on a book that would describe some of the powerful healing techniques I had seen. Although I often thought of asking Myra about writing her story, I couldn't discuss it with her. After all, I had never had anything published, and she had been the subject of magazine articles and had twice been featured on national TV.

One day, as I was concluding a visit with her, she turned to me and said, "You know why we met, don't you?"

"No, not really," I responded.

She looked at me and smiled. "You're supposed to write my story."

I almost lost my breath. It was more than I could have imagined, more than I could have asked for. "I'd love to," I said.

My experiences with Myra have been nothing short of remarkable. She apparently knew I would be able to help her write this book long before I did, and strangely, even before I had told her I was attempting to become a writer.

I spent the next several months meeting with her, making dozens of pages of notes and filling many hours of cassette tapes, but for me the work had just begun, a work that would be interrupted many times. I often apologized to Myra for allowing myself to become distracted from her book; and in typical Myra fashion, she would respond, "Don't worry. The book will be completed when both you and it are ready."

My being ready wasn't something I had contemplated; and it would take several years before I could properly describe the experiences she shared with me. However, the delays provided time to learn even more about this very special woman. Myra Starr is a powerful healer with extraordinary gifts, most of which I learned about only through intense questioning, for she never flaunted her abilities or accomplishments; and it was obvious that she had no desire for celebrity. During one of my last taping sessions, she remarked casually, "If this book is successful, I'm not interested in traveling. You'll have to do any interviews."

Myra's simple but powerful message of love and compassion is why I felt it so important to tell her story. There is another dimension out there—a world of angels and healing that can bring us to a better understanding of both ourselves and the life we often perceive as overwhelming. The messages the angels send are of hope and encouragement. If only a few will listen, we can heal both ourselves and our planet.

Although her story is remarkable, and at times may seem unbelievable, it is even more astounding than I have been able to record. I sense the inadequacy of my words to convey what the angels shared with her. My experiences with Myra, and others she described, are far more powerful than can be expressed in a few short pages. My hope is that her words will somehow awaken the reader to the powerful and loving energy she brought back from the angels, the same that resides within each of us.

Be aware as you read, for the angels are also speaking to you. Listen to your inner guides, to the Source of all that is, for you may discover your true self. As you share in Myra's experiences, she sends her prayers and wishes that you may find the peace that comes through understanding. And like seeds cast upon a wind, such awareness blossoms and spreads across the land.

The following pages reveal the story of Myra Starr, a story of hope, encouragement and incredible love. It has been written just as she told it to me. I have been no more than a vehicle through which the angels and guides have shared their healing message. I am grateful for having participated in this wondrous journey and honored that she and her guides chose me to record it.

John Mulkey
July, 2011

CHAPTER 1

The Journey Begins

I hardly noticed the wailing siren as the ambulance carried me through the narrow streets of my neighborhood. It didn't seem real. The Emergency Medical Technician (EMT) tried to get my attention. "Ma'am, can you hear me?" I knew the question was for me, but I couldn't answer. Strangely, I didn't care.

The coach bounced violently, and several items spilled from an overhead compartment. Must be the railroad crossing, I thought. Now we'll turn onto Main Street. The young man above me leaned over, bracing himself against the side of the vehicle. "We're losing her," he yelled.

Struggling to maintain his balance, the technician grabbed my arm and tried to insert a needle. "Stay with me," he said.

I didn't want to stay—I didn't want anything. For a moment I tried to understand, but I was dying. I didn't have to understand. I was relieved death was coming so easily.

I looked onto the scene from a bizarre vantage point. It had been the same when the EMTs had first arrived. From high overhead I had watched as they worked on my body, lying on the bedroom floor. I saw what the young man was doing, saw the person he was working on—me. But I didn't question how I could see everything, and I wasn't concerned about what was happening. If I was dying, that would be the end of it.

The young man was still poking my arm with a needle. Though his movements were rough, I felt no pain, no sensation at all, for I was no longer in the body on which he worked so feverishly. I watched from some strange dimension, disconnected, yet drawn to the scene with bizarre curiosity. I wanted to see, to know what was happening, and to understand. The feeling of being an observer, the same as in so many times past, filled me with wonder.

Unlike those other experiences, I wasn't dreaming. There was a powerful difference, and though I couldn't identify exactly what it was, I feared the reality of my experience. Hovering just above the scene, I watched events that were to change my life forever.

The technician continued his struggle, searching for a vein that had not yet collapsed, and I sensed his frustration. A wave of compassion flowed through me as I watched his futile attempts to save a life. Though some part of me felt a slight connection to the body convulsing on the gurney, I was more concerned for the young man and how he would feel about his failed efforts. The patient was becoming a stranger, and I watched as one might watch a play, interested, but without emotion.

The siren continued as the ambulance careened down the highway. Through the rear window I could see my husband, Mike, his hands spinning the wheel from side to side in a desperate effort to keep pace. I saw his face clearly, sensed his fear, his anguish, felt the panic that filled his mind.

"She's not going to make it," the technician yelled out once more. He pounded her chest. Moments later his voice lowered. "It's no use. She's gone." He reached down and pulled a sheet over a face that had, in a different time, belonged to me.

I wasn't concerned for the body disappearing under the crisp white covering, for what I'd once thought of as "me" was becoming "her," a meaningless and lifeless shell of no further use. It could be discarded like an old coat, once comfortable, but frayed and worn, and represented only a minute and insignificant part of a life that was gone. The new me, without the limits of a body, was overwhelmed in an amazing sense of power and freedom as waves of energy poured into each cell.

Everything was clear, but I could see much more than my surroundings, more than a mere picture. I saw what made things as they were. It was as if I could tap into the minds of others and know their thoughts. Once more I looked to the man driving close behind. The shock would be terrible. His connection to the draped corpse was still strong.

"Don't do it," I pleaded. "Don't let her husband see her like that. Uncover her. He can't lose hope now."

The young man ignored my cries and leaned forward to talk with the driver. Why couldn't I make him hear me? Through the rear window I saw fear on the face in the windshield. I had to do something.

I mustered all my strength, all my will, and with phantom hands, reached down to the technician's arm. "Please uncover her." I tried to force the words to form. The young man jerked from my spectral grasp and shook his head. I was pleased as he grabbed the edge of the sheet, folded it back, and neatly tucked it under her chin. And though the features were swollen and grotesquely distorted, I felt better knowing Mike would see her face as they wheeled her into the emergency room.

Uncovering the face seemed to trigger what happened next. As soon as the covering was pulled back, my mind exploded with a tremendous flash. Torn from my vantage point, I passed through the side of the ambulance and hurled through space toward a sphere of white light. In an instant I was gone. I was in one place one moment, then another, vastly different, in a second or less. And it was there in the brilliance of a thousand stars, I saw God.

I remember the cold—a hard metallic cold—that was different from winter. It came from inside me, and I couldn't stop the trembling. An unpleasant mix of strong odors and unrecognizable sounds came at me from all sides. Bright light penetrated my eyelids. Where was I and what was going on? At the time it didn't occur to me to open my eyes.

A voice called out, "Honey, we need to get you to a room. Try to wake up." Icy fingers brushed across my forehead, and my eyes sprang open. The blurred figure of a woman leaned over and wrapped something around my arm.

I grabbed her hand and pulled her to me. "Teach what?" I tried to speak, but the words spilled out as incomprehensible gibberish—I'd later learn that my jaw had been shattered during my convulsions—and the pain was intense. "Who am I supposed to teach? I don't even have a degree."

The woman gasped and stumbled backwards as items crashed from a bedside tray.

"What the . . . I guess you are awake." She stepped near me and laughed. "Don't you worry. You're going to be okay now, but you sure gave us a scare. Rest. I'll come back and check on you in a few minutes." She turned to walk away.

Her words failed to comfort me. I wasn't okay. The room was blurred and I couldn't bring my eyes into focus—a check with an ophthalmologist would confirm that the experience had changed my once 20/20 vision to the point where bifocals would be needed.

"What happened?" I mumbled. "How did I get here?"

"You had a seizure, maybe a reaction to something. Your husband said you'd been taking allergy medicine. That could have been it."

My original question persisted. "Teach what?"

The last thing I remembered was an incredible dream where I was surrounded by angels. "Now you must return," they had said. "You will teach and heal."

My mind began to retrace the steps of that morning, November 11, 1989. I recalled getting up, showering, and preparing my medication. After taking the syringe from the drawer, I'd inserted it into a vial of serum, the same stuff I'd taken for months. There was nothing unusual about that.

Beyond that point my normal morning routine faded into a blur, overshadowed by powerful and bizarre events. What could have triggered the incident? The injections I took were practically foolproof, and I had done them for almost a year. It was unlikely I'd made a mistake. Had there been a problem with the medicine? I'd drawn from a new bottle. Could it have been contaminated? None of it made sense.

Whatever had happened, something had taken me through the doors of death. And though I had heard of near-death experiences, I always considered them fantasies, hallucinations—as some have speculated—caused by a brain starved for oxygen. My visions, however, defied explanation. They were real.

There was another strange and unusual element of the event, a series of coincidences that caused me to wonder if there could be some special purpose. If Mike had not been home, for instance, I'm sure I would have died and lain there on the bedroom floor until he returned that evening. A weekday would have almost ensured my death for he always left for work long before I did.

I had told him earlier in the week that I had been asked to work that Saturday, and though he wasn't required to, in the past he had always chosen to work those times I did. His boss had even come by the night before to see if he would be available.

"Absolutely not!" Mike had answered.

His terse response had surprised me. It wasn't like him. But he offered no explanation, and I didn't bother to ask. What had urged him to remain home that morning? I puzzled over that question and others as the bizarre events surrounding my death experience began to sink in.

By the time the paramedics had arrived, Mike would later tell me, I was convulsing. But I had seen them. In our bedroom I watched as they worked on my body—at that time I still thought of it as my body—although I remember that I later thought of it simply as "her." Of course it was strange, but I wasn't focused upon my unusual powers of vision; I wanted to know what had happened. Where had I gone?

I didn't remember separating from my body, but at some point I realized I was looking down on everything. I could see the paramedics trying to resuscitate me, searching for signs of life.

From the moment they had begun I had known their efforts were wasted.

The most startling part of the experience, however, was what happened in the ambulance when they uncovered my face. At that moment I began a wonderful and ecstatic journey. As the covering slid away, it was as if a doorway opened allowing me to escape, and I immediately passed through the side of the ambulance and into the brightest light I'd ever seen. I didn't experience the tunnel that some have described, and had no idea where I was going.

My understanding of time in that other dimension is one aspect that still bothers me. While many parts of the odyssey seemed to have happened in seconds, when I think about them, they expand to infinity. My journey into the light happened in the blink of an eye, yet in some altered form of slow motion that allowed me to absorb a tremendous amount of information.

The experience was disorienting. There were no things or places as I'd once experienced, no up or down, left or right. Everything came from the marvelous light which was both transporting and consuming me. Its unimaginable brilliance penetrated to the core of my soul, surrounding me, drawing me into a vortex of incredible power and energy. I was in the wonderful presence of God!

I didn't see a being, didn't see a form; the light was all there was. A voice called my name, a voice I knew to be that of God. I was awed by His presence and one with all things. I had no fear, surrounded by an overwhelming awareness of being loved. No human could ever express the depth of love I felt that day, yet I continue to be comforted in the knowledge that such love can be showered upon us.

A marvelous symphony and chorus vibrated to the core of my being, celestial music the finest orchestra cannot equal. The sound was soothing, penetrating, and filled me with joy. The vibrations cradled me and opened my mind to an awareness of life I had never before considered. At once I was both the listener and the music as a feeling of total peace and acceptance swept over me. I didn't think or analyze; I experienced.

Beings of pure light that I can best describe as angelic showed me events from my past—a life review of sorts. I saw times when I could have brought love and joy to those around me. In selfishness and fear I had failed. I was saddened as I realized what might have been.

I didn't just recall how I had felt; I relived feelings and emotions from others too. It was as if I became them. I knew their thoughts and felt their pain.

The angels were aware of the smallest and most insignificant details of my life. They showed me how each event has importance far beyond what we see on the surface. My actions had touched others in ways I had never imagined and reached people I had never met. Most of the scenes passed by quickly, but a few paused before me, allowing me to relive experiences long forgotten.

One such event was a childhood visit with my grandmother, a kind and gentle woman whose Cherokee heritage had taught her love and respect for all of nature. I saw myself at about age six being guided through her garden. She lovingly talked about each plant, how they provided food, medicine, and beauty. We walked into her rose garden where she explained how each one was different, with different needs, and how each was unique in its gift to us.

As the angels took me back through that experience, I understood the importance of my willingness to listen and learn. I loved being with my grandmother and would have enjoyed anything she wanted to share with me, but for her that time seemed especially significant. She had received great satisfaction from the interest of a child and was encouraged that one so young would take time to listen and learn. Seeing that event helped me understand how we can bring happiness to others just by listening, that our interest in the simplest of things can touch, even change, lives.

Words and deeds have great power, and I saw the importance of how I respond to those around me. A smile given to a stranger, a kind word to someone at the checkout counter, a simple compliment, or a gesture of respect can bring peace and joy to both the giver and receiver.

With loving care I was guided through other events, some painful, most long since released from memory. The angels offered no judgment and there was no punishment. Criticism was unnecessary, as I immediately understood how I had misused my life. The visions consumed me, opening me to an awareness I had never before experienced. I had been guided by a loving and divine presence that had watched over me, yet allowing me the freedom to be whatever I chose.

It was perfectly clear why I was shown my past. The vision was an expression of love, a connection with what was real and meaningful, presented to awaken me to my true self and rid me of fear of the afterlife. The hell I had imagined and sometimes experienced, existed only in my mind, and the horrors I envisioned were, at the most, meaningless. I watched, fascinated, but without comment from my ego, as a moving picture unfolded before me.

I saw how all things are connected, how the impact of our actions reach far beyond those with whom we come in contact. I understood how words and actions touch others in ways we've never imagined, how the seemingly insignificant sometimes affects a lifetime. The energy patterns formed in a thought can generate an ever-expanding spiral of influence that will spread across the globe. Each wave of the spiral interacts with those of others, creating new and unimagined consequences. I had never before considered the power we wield.

I once read how a butterfly flapping its wings on one side of the globe can spawn a hurricane thousands of miles away. What the angels showed me helped me to understand that statement. There is a web of life. Each strand, regardless of how small, touches another, and each strand has the power to alter the web in ways our limited awareness can't begin to comprehend.

An awakening stirred within me, as if I'd come from the deepest of sleeps, and I was able to view life in a way I'd never done before. My mind was freed of its limitations, and I saw beyond the surface of events into what was real and meaningful.

My enhanced vision showed me the meaning of family, how we create the bonds that tie us all together. Families are not merely those connected in blood, but are for us to create as we draw others to us who share in our beliefs and commitments. Those true kinsmen provide a mutual support system that allows each to discover their source of power and energy. More importantly, they enshroud the world in prayers, not limited by their wishes for others, but reaching for the highest good in every situation.

Then, in what can best be described as a slide show, I saw a combined vision of the past and future and received a mass of information and instruction beyond comprehension. It was as if a giant computer suddenly downloaded its files into my brain.

I was aware that I received the information, but strangely unaware of its content. Even as it was happening I couldn't focus on a single part. Later, I would think about the experience to see if I could recall anything from the downloading, but I couldn't force it to come. It was like those times when we awaken and know we've had a dream, and yet, can't remember any of the details.

Though I didn't understand the information I was receiving, I had a sense of storing massive amounts of data that were immediately locked from my conscious awareness. The sensation was overwhelming, intoxicating, and gave me a strange feeling of power.

I wasn't afraid of what had happened; I had an intense desire to know more. There was a magical, almost transcendent quality to the experience, but not everything was positive. Because I didn't understand what had happened, I considered a series of options. None offered much promise. I was desperate to know, wondering if I were losing my mind. The most acceptable scenario was that it was just another of my crazy dreams. I wanted to believe so. What else could it have been?

I knew it would be best to forget the whole ordeal, but the more I tried, the more I wondered why. If there had been some purpose, I had no idea what it was. Though some of the visions had been beautiful, they had only served to create frustration and anxiety. I wondered what would happen next. The answer would come sooner than expected.

CHAPTER 2

Angel Encounters

More than three weeks had passed since my deliverance from death, yet I was no closer to understanding what had happened than when it all began. The experience had left me confused, struggling to comprehend, and I continually felt as if something terrible was going to happen. I should have been ecstatic; I could have died. Instead, I was haunted by visions and memories my rational self told me were impossible, and none of it made sense.

My ordeal had begun that Saturday morning at about seven o'clock, minutes after I'd given myself a routine allergy injection. I'd grown accustomed to the shots, didn't mind the brief sting; and though I'd been taking them for months, that morning, something went terribly wrong.

The doctors never were quite sure—at least never admitted—what had happened, but my body reacted violently as an allergic reaction shut down my internal systems. I was fortunate to have survived. Even the EMTs that responded to my husband's frantic call were sure I wouldn't make it. Long before we reached the hospital, they had given up.

My life had been saved by a stranger; an emergency room physician, whose persistence and dedication had given me one more chance to live. In the months to come, I would consider a more startling possibility.

Each day filled me with new anxieties. Though I could deal with the parts I understood—I'd never feared death—the rest of it was frightening. My mind was racked by fears from an unknown dimension, and I struggled to discover the meaning of what had happened. The answers wouldn't come. Seeking comfort from the normalcy that had existed only a few weeks before, I tried to lose myself in my work. Even that didn't help. What had once given me a sense of worth no longer provided satisfaction. Unable to maintain my focus, my job would become increasingly difficult, practically impossible.

I poured myself a cup of coffee, eased into my favorite chair, and gazed out the window. Outside, a brisk autumn wind enticed the few remaining leaves from their branches. Beyond the patio the wall of trees that only a couple of months earlier had sheltered me from the summer's heat stood naked, a line of impotent sentries unable to halt the advancing rays. I kicked off my slippers and bathed my feet in the cozy blanket of light. The sun's rays glistened against the window, a shimmering mirror on which I projected my thoughts.

I took a few sips of coffee and placed the cup on the small table beside my chair. Leaning back I searched for peace in the quiet of the morning's calm. There was none to be found. No matter how I tried, I couldn't release the impending sense of dread that blanketed my thoughts. Something was happening, something beyond comprehension, and it gnawed at my insides.

My death experience was a bombshell that had shaken me to the core, but that wasn't what troubled me. I'd been near death before, years earlier, when the doctors said I might not survive cancer surgery. No, what bothered me, the haunting vision I couldn't forget, was what had happened, the things I had seen and the strange places I visited after the EMS technicians thought I was dead. That's what I couldn't get out of my mind.

I reached down to the table and picked up my notebook to begin organizing my day, a habit I had followed each morning for as long as I could remember. With the notebook on my lap, I tried to focus on my schedule, pressing the pen to the paper. Nothing happened. The pen was frozen. Some unseen force had taken control of my body. Regardless of how hard I tried, I couldn't make it move. I attempted to take another sip of coffee, but my muscles failed to respond.

Without warning everything around me began to spin as if I'd been swept into a cyclone. My pad and pen slipped to the floor. I squeezed hard on the chair's arm in an attempt to halt the dizzying movements. My fingers passed through empty air. There was no chair! It had vanished along with the room where I'd been seated.

My brain exploded as if struck by lightning. I wanted to scream. I thought I was having a stroke. For what seemed like hours, I couldn't move, couldn't see, blinded by something terrible going on inside my head.

After a time my vision began to return, imperceptibly at first, then I became aware of a pale light around me. Soon, I could see vague shapes. I had no doubt I was still in my living room, poised to make out my schedule, but as my sight cleared, I received the most startling vision of all. I wasn't in my chair. I wasn't even in my house! Muscles tightened as adrenaline surged through my body, and my heart thundered against the walls of my chest. With no idea of where I was or what was happening, my mind waged an impossible battle to understand. Before it could come up with an answer, my senses told me what my mind couldn't accept. I was underground—in a tunnel or cave!

Those who have been underground know what I mean. You can feel it, hear it, smell it. The unbearable silence is so thick you can touch it. The dark recesses of the inner earth hold an aura of mystery that envelops all who enter. Once experienced, such places are impossible to forget.

The cool dampness that surrounded me penetrated my blouse. I shivered, wrapping my arms tight against my chest. The trembling increased, not so much because of the cold, but more from the uncontrolled and frenzied beating of my heart. Short gulps of musty air surged into my lungs, and I tried to calm myself by breathing more slowly. The thick vapor was stale, yet strangely sweet. As it flowed into my body, it magically seemed to relax each cell. After a few breaths my heart slowed, and I let out a long sigh.

It may seem strange that I was able to compose myself, for my situation was bizarre beyond description. Where was I? I knew I couldn't be in a cave, but I couldn't imagine why it seemed I was. What was happening?

I bit my lip until I tasted blood. The sharp pain convinced me I wasn't dreaming. As my mind tried to rationalize the unimaginable, I breathed slowly while some unknown faculty kept me from panic.

I looked around, desperate for an explanation. In the semi-darkness I could hardly see, but as my eyes adjusted, I noticed tiny sparkles of light surrounding me on all sides. The light came from small crystals embedded in the walls of the cave. There were thousands, perhaps millions, of the tiny lights, their faint glow providing barely enough light to see.

I tried to step forward but couldn't. The only muscles that responded were my eyes. They darted back and forth surveying the scene before me. One side of my brain argued that I had to be dreaming, while the other tried to show why that couldn't be. I had never had a dream so strange, one where I could smell, hear, and feel.

I focused all my attention to my right hand and attempted to reach out. Though it couldn't move, I did feel a slight tingling and movement in my fingers. I flexed them back and forth, relishing in a minute but comforting amount of control over my body. After a few moments I was startled by the sudden motion of my hand as it made a few erratic movements towards the wall, slowly at first, then more rapidly until it made contact. I pressed my palm against the cold dampness beside me, sliding my fingers into tiny crevices. The sensations made me certain of one thing. I was awake. But where I was and how I'd come there were questions I couldn't answer.

The movement of my hand encouraged me. I tested my legs to see if they would work too. One at a time I lifted my feet. I was sure I could force myself to walk, however slow it might be. But where would I go? I had no idea where I was or how to get home. Recalling that morning still brings chills. I can't begin to describe the emotions, questions, and confusion I felt. I didn't know if I should try to move or not and wondered what I would find if I did.

At some point I noticed sounds—the crackling of a fire and what at first seemed to be a low hum, but later sounded like distant voices. I crouched low to avoid being seen, peering into the semi-darkness trying to determine if anyone was approaching. When no one appeared, I inched forward along a narrow passage coming to an abrupt halt when it opened into a large cavern. In the center a small fire burned, its flickering glow allowing me to see more clearly. Beyond the fire, under a massive rock overhang, a young woman, dressed in animal skin clothing, was leaning over the trembling body of a child. Their appearance was that of Native Americans, but they looked to be from another time. In the shadows behind the two I saw two others, adults who were dressed the same and who appeared to be watching the woman.

I'm familiar with the term "Indians;" my father was Cherokee. As a young girl I heard the taunts from children towards those whose appearance was different from their own. The strange group before me rekindled uncomfortable memories from the past, how I had concealed my heritage for years, embarrassed by my connection to a culture that was generally misunderstood and often ridiculed.

The young woman before me seemed to be giving treatment to the child. I stared, fixated on the scene as if it were real, but knowing it had to be a dream, a fantasy created in my mind. No other possibility was acceptable.

Could my medication have triggered such a series of fantastic hallucinations? My awareness told me no, reminding me of the powerful sensations I felt. Everything was too real to be a dream or delusion.

The setting was bizarre and frightening, engulfing me in a mysterious labyrinth. I was trapped by circumstances I could neither understand nor control. Though one part of me was terrified, fearing I had lost my mind, something deep inside calmed me and filled me with peace. The place had a familiar presence to it. I'd been there before.

While I watched from the shadows, the young woman continued her work with the child, a girl no more than seven years old. I sensed the woman was a healer. Although I was unfamiliar with what she was doing, I knew she was performing some type of healing ritual, and her methods seemed strangely appropriate. I watched with the intensity of a medical student observing her first surgery.

Concealing myself in a small alcove, I breathed slowly; only the slightest whisper escaped. An inner awareness, however, told me the woman sensed my presence. I shivered with the possibility of detection, pressing my body ever tighter against the cool dampness beside me, but I was unable to turn away, captivated by my strange vision. Though the healer gave no indication she had seen me, I was sure I'd been discovered.

The child was frightened and occasionally made low whimpering sounds. I sensed she was in pain. In the flickering light I saw a few cuts and bruises, but I somehow knew she had other wounds, invisible to me, injuries to her hip and leg. As the healer continued, she focused on those areas, singing a wondrous melody that calmed both me and the child. After a time the child grew silent, and I could see her chest rising and falling as she breathed in slow, deep, rhythmic breaths.

There was an aura of light and color radiating above the child. I've never seen the body's energy, wasn't even sure I believed it could be seen, but I immediately and inexplicably knew that was what I was seeing. A soft, slightly blurred light extended several inches from her body. The light glowed with faint colors, but was gathered into thick gray masses around the injuries.

I was fascinated as the healer moved her hands about. The child's energy responded to her movements with changes in color and intensity. I studied each action and watched as she placed small stones around and on the child's body. She put several on the chest, one in each hand, while others were lined at her side. The stones also affected the energy, and the healer used them to focus the flow coming from her hands.

At times she changed the position of the stones, added others, and held her hands still, as if intensifying the force in certain areas. As she worked, the child's aura became brighter, the gray disappeared, and the color equalized all around her body.

Watching the healing process caused my fears to vanish, and I leaned forward. Something called to me. I stepped from the shadows, enchanted by the fantastic phenomena I'd observed. The healer looked up and smiled, motioning for me to join her. I knew she had been waiting for me.

She told me her name was Maya (pronounced Māya), although the information I received was not in words. We experienced perfect communication through our thoughts, with an instantaneous awareness of everything the other wished to say. As it was happening, the process seemed perfectly normal, and I never questioned my unusual ability to understand her.

Looking back, it seems strange that I didn't think about the similarity of our names. I suppose I was too busy taking in all that I was seeing, but I've often wondered if the two of us are more connected than I might imagine.

Maya told me she would teach me the ways of healing. As soon as I received her message, I was instantly aware that I could see through her eyes. Through her vision I looked inside the body of the child!

She showed me how to interpret the energy body and explained how she had used her hands to balance the flow. The experience was both wonderful and disturbing, but was only a brief preview of things to come.

Each movement, each message from the healer fascinated me, and I stood in awe, absorbing her thoughts and filling my mind with healing techniques that seemed as old as time itself. I received new insights into life, savoring each bit of knowledge as it flowed effortlessly into my awareness. As I watched and listened, an ever-strengthening bond joined the two of us together.

Once her work with the child was complete, the experience ended abruptly, and I was instantly transported back to my living room, pen and pad on the floor at my feet, a cup of cold coffee at my side. It seemed as if hours had passed, but my clock told me I had been gone little more than an hour.

When I think about that first encounter, I can't imagine why I didn't offer more objections, didn't question why I was there, and didn't ask: Why me? Instead, while in the presence of the healer, I accepted the experience as normal.

As soon as I began to recall the morning's events, however, the reality of the situation settled in. Once more I was filled with fear. I couldn't have been in a cave, couldn't have had the experiences, regardless of how real they seemed. It wasn't possible. I didn't know what to make of it.

Long-forgotten memories from my childhood came to mind. There had been other times of strange visions and experiences, things I had been told not to discuss. I had long tried to block them from memory, and for the most part, I'd been successful. Were they returning?

One thing seemed certain. Whatever had occurred probably wasn't good. And I wouldn't be able to tell anyone; I knew better. Everyone would think I was crazy. Mother had warned me about that.

CHAPTER 3

My Connection with the Unseen

My first exposure to the spirit world came when I was five years old. It was about that time when I began to experience unusual and vivid dreams; and the strangest part of all was that they occasionally came true. In my dreams I felt as if I were in a bubble, watching everything around me but separate and unable to participate. I would sometimes awaken shivering, enveloped in an incredible coldness, and always remembering the most minute details. Many of those dreams were about insignificant parts of my life, encounters with relatives and visions of places and people I'd never seen. Most were uninteresting and especially boring to a young girl. Although some came true, I paid them little attention.

A few of my dreams, however, were special and more interesting, some even remarkable. When I would awaken I would know that something extraordinary was going to happen. The same feeling of coldness would come over me, and I would be unusually alert with a vivid memory of everything I had dreamed. Those dreams and the accompanying sensations seemed to be a signal of what was to come. Those dreams always came true.

The first time I told my mother about the experiences, she warned me not to repeat what I had told her, forbidding me from discussing such matters with anyone When she realized how many of my dreams were coming true, she seemed frightened. "Never speak of such nonsense again," she said. "If you do, I will call people who will come and take you away."

Her harsh words and the thought of being separated from my family tormented me, so I tried to suppress the dreams, especially ignoring those that left me with the special feeling. I never mentioned them to her again. My refusal to give them attention made the dreams less frequent, and I grew older with the belief that the strange visions had been unnatural, caused by an affliction not to be discussed.

From time to time, however, the nights would still bring insights into the future. When I was eight I dreamed of stepping on a snake. In my dream I was walking in the tall grass behind our house and felt something move under my foot. I looked down as a large brown snake raised its head and wriggled across my foot. Though it seems odd, I wasn't afraid, somehow aware that it wasn't poisonous, but I couldn't move, held fast by an irresistible force. In my vision I was fascinated as the reptile wrapped its cool, pulsing body around my ankle and lower leg. I awoke with a vivid memory of all that had happened.

A few days later my encounter with the snake occurred, just as I had seen it, and once again I wasn't afraid. My dream had prepared me, and I let the snake perform its ritual, waiting patiently until it slid into the bushes. Although I had not felt fear, the vision made a lasting impression. I became forever aware of the unique and prophetic nature of some of the dreams.

As I grew older I realized that my experiences weren't limited to my dreamtime. On occasion I experienced *déjà vu*, and I had frequent premonitions about phone calls that would come. I could sometimes sense when the phone was about to ring and know who was calling before answering. I even had premonitions about letters that were to arrive in the mail. Occasionally, when meeting new people, I would receive insights into their personality or beliefs, and based upon those insights I would develop immediate and strong feelings of like or dislike about them. Often their subsequent actions would show me that what I had felt was correct.

I had also developed the ability to tell whether or not people were telling the truth. During the year I worked for a placement agency, that talent was especially useful. As job seekers described their educational history and work experience, I would immediately know if they were being truthful. After verifying a few of my insights, I began to rely on my feelings to assist in my work.

When I was in my early twenties, I had my first vision from the past. I was dating Dave, a divorcé with three small children, and had developed a close relationship with him. His kind and gentle manner coupled with his devotion to his children made him appear to be an ideal choice for a mate. I was further impressed by his commitment to his faith. Though I lacked the depth of religious training he had, I was sure his beliefs provided a sound foundation for marriage. It would be much later when I would discover how religious teachings alone are not the best indication of one's true spirituality, and I would struggle to understand the closed minds that a limited religious outlook can sometimes foster.

As my relationship with Dave grew, I learned more about his life and was drawn even closer to him. I learned how he had suffered the tragedy of losing a child, killed in a freak auto accident. Dave felt responsible, having insisted that the boy accompany him as he delivered the morning papers. I later learned that the children were required to take turns helping with the newspaper delivery, a job intended to build character.

I knew few details of the accident for Dave never discussed it. What I did know, I learned from friends who spoke of the incident in hushed tones. I sensed not to ask questions, and instead maintained a constant series of activities to divert his attention.

Life was unfolding as I had always dreamed it would, and soon Dave asked me to marry. I eagerly accepted. I was excited about beginning a family, and with his three children I would have a head start.

In December, on his deceased son's birthday, I joined the family as they visited the grave site. At the cemetery, the youngest child, a daughter, stepped forward to place a bouquet at her brother's headstone. As she leaned over, she paused and handed me one of the flowers.

When she stepped back, I knelt before the marker and reached to place my lone flower in the vase. As I did, my body jerked as if a surge of electricity passed through me. The shock was so violent that I staggered backward, almost falling.

That night I had one of my special dreams and awoke sitting in bed with the familiar coldness I'd experienced so many times during my childhood. Every detail of the boy's death appeared to me in brilliant color. It was as if the entire event had been shown to me, but at the same time I also felt I was there. I saw the green overalls and bright yellow shirt the child had worn on the day of the accident, the ball he had asked to take with him in the car. I watched the two pull out of the driveway and turn into the morning sun, heard the screech of tires as the car skidded to avoid debris in the road. I felt the sickening crash as the car slammed into a parked truck, its cargo tearing through the windshield and crushing the child.

In my dream I heard Dave's anguished cries as he held his dying son, and I watched the rescue workers futile efforts to save him. The vision continued as I re-lived the funeral and saw the tiny body dressed in a blue suit and tie and placed in a coffin lined with sky-blue fabric.

From another dimension the spirit of the boy came to me. Though he appeared as a child, I sensed wisdom and uncommon awareness. "Daddy won't understand," he said, "but please tell him I'm happy. There is no reason to be sad. I didn't die. Tell him grandpa is here, and Uncle Ted, too."

I sat in bed trembling, hardly able to contain my excitement. Once I had composed myself, I called Dave and told him I had wonderful news. We arranged to meet the following day. I was eager to share my vision and the message from his son, but I wanted to tell him in person. When we met I described my experience at the cemetery and began to give him the details of my dream. I told him how I had seen the accident, and that his son had spoken to me.

Dave stopped me in mid sentence. His eyes grew wide and he stared at me with a look of contempt. His expression told me all I needed to know. He didn't share my excitement and didn't want to know more. Instead, he reacted with anger.

"You're a witch," he yelled. "But you won't get me with your sorcery. I know what you're doing, and it won't work with me."

I stepped back in horror. The words were more than I could bear. My only wish had been to share the positive side of my experience. I had never considered it might be interpreted differently. A vision of my mother flashed before me. Her warnings not to discuss such things had proven true. She had been right all along.

Dave pointed his finger at me. "I never want to see you again. If you see me on the street, don't even look my way. You're working with the devil."

I drove home, more determined than ever to lock away my abilities forever. Perhaps I was bewitched, or worse, insane. I wasn't sure. But it seemed obvious that people would not accept my visions. I wanted to forget the strange dreams, the messages, and live a normal life. What I had was not a gift, but an evil curse that drove others away.

It would take months for me to begin to overcome what had happened with Dave. The event had left me hurt and confused. With an expectation of strengthening our relationship, I'd been unprepared for what had happened. My senses were numbed, and I drifted from one day to the next without thinking or caring about the future.

In my efforts to focus my thoughts away from the incident I was aided by a powerful distraction. In early autumn I became ill. In the weeks that followed, the good health and boundless energy I'd once enjoyed, faded into a nightmare of pain and fatigue. At first the doctors didn't seem to know what was wrong, but they later agreed on the source of my problems. "Just a couple of small growths," one doctor had said. "They're pretty common. A hysterectomy would be one option, but that should be the last consideration. You're much too young. You'll want to have children. Let's see what we can do with medication."

I had always assumed I would have children, hoping to one day create the kind of family life I had missed, and the medication route seemed to make sense. I agreed, eager to get rid of the pain and nausea that had become a part of each day.

That fall and winter seemed the longest of my life. There were times I was too sick to get out of bed. When the medicine didn't help, I tried another doctor. He, too, was reluctant to perform surgery and gave me a prescription for a drug that had just recently been approved. The pain did ease up somewhat, but the nausea grew worse.

My mounting fear and depression led me to call Tom, an old friend who had stood by me during some of my most difficult times. His willingness to listen to my problem rekindled a relationship from several years earlier. The kind of friend girls often have between serious relationships, he was someone to confide in, to seek advice from, but for me, not to marry. Sure we were close, but I saw him differently from the other men I dated. He seemed more like a brother. When I wanted to talk he was there, and when I needed space, he knew to back away.

One of the most sensitive men I've ever known, Tom is probably the least appreciated. I'm sure I often took his devotion and caring attitude for granted, and his willingness to overlook my faults encouraged me to continue. An officer in the Air Force, he could also be described as one of the most persistent people I've ever known. That single trait is what eventually caused me to succumb to his never-ending proposals.

"I know you don't love me the way I love you," he sometimes said. "But you do care about me and know I'll do whatever it takes to make you happy. You've always been my sweetheart."

He was right. Our feelings were not the same, but I sometimes wondered if I was so different that I was unable to experience emotions as others did.

When he was transferred to Iran a few months later, I thought I wouldn't have to deal with the question. He was gone and I would go on with my life. Tom had a different idea. As soon as he was settled in Tehran, he began writing every week.

"Come to Iran," he pleaded. "You'll love it."

I replied to each letter, not wanting to hurt his feelings. The thousands of miles separating us seemed a sufficient barrier to protect me, but as time passed, our long distance relationship grew. My health was still a problem, and I'm sure my letters conveyed my deepening depression. After a few months I received a package from him. The letter inside read, "Open me first."

"Marry me," it began. The letter outlined detailed plans he had made for me to join him in Iran. "I promise you the best medical treatment the Air Force can offer and to allow you the freedom I know you need."

The small box inside contained an engagement ring. A note was attached. "If this fits, then you have to say yes."

The ring fit perfectly and the offer more than I could refuse. I didn't try to analyze. I called him and accepted.

A month later I joined him and we were married a few weeks after that. Marriage made it easier to forget the pains of my past. My health even seemed to improve as I busied myself setting up a new household in a small apartment we had located on the outskirts of Tehran. Because I wasn't working, I spent long hours creating a fantasied vision of the life I hoped to be unfolding for me. And though I didn't always feel great, my body adjusted to the nausea I sometimes felt, and most of the time I could block out the illness that continued to plague me. For the first time in my life, I'd been accepted for who I was.

As the excitement of the move faded and the realities of marriage settled in, I found it increasingly difficult to ignore the old signals from my body. I tired easily and many days was too weak to leave the house. While I tried to hide my concerns, hoping my condition would miraculously improve, Tom knew something was wrong. He insisted I go to the doctor. "I'm sure you're okay, too, but it's a good idea to check with the experts."

A friend recommended an Iranian doctor that she had used, and I scheduled an appointment. After conducting little more than a superficial examination, he made his diagnosis. "I think you have an ulcer," he said. "Perhaps our food is not agreeing with you. I can prescribe some medication."

Along with my prescription drugs, I took some over-the-counter medicines suggested by one of my well-meaning friends. The combination created a numbing effect that allowed me to function. Tehran also proved to be an alluring ally, providing a wealth of diversions from my pain.

For a time I enjoyed the new and exciting life the city offered. Exploring its many facets kept me busy for weeks. On days I felt well enough I would tour the city and surrounding countryside, and I began to love the country, its heritage, and its remarkable people.

Our landlords, a couple of moderate wealth and status, lived in a large apartment below us. I sometimes spent the afternoons with their beautiful daughter, Elohe, with whom I had made an agreement. I would help her improve her English and she would teach me to speak Farsi, the language of Iran.

Educated in London with a broad knowledge of world affairs, Elohe was a delight to be with. Her understanding of government policies, especially those of the United States, was surprising and at times, embarrassing. Though she didn't view us as "ugly Americans," she was well aware of our involvement in her country.

"I fear for what may come," she once confided. Your government can not ignore what is happening here. There are powerful forces in opposition to our present leadership. The future does not look good for either of us."

I had heard of occasional disturbances, but I assumed them to be the work of a few radicals who opposed the Shah. And I never felt threatened when I went into the bazaar. Of course my dark hair and skin made it easier for me to go unnoticed than some of my fair-skinned friends.

My first year living in Iran seemed like an extended vacation. From visits to the Caspian Sea, to camping in the desert, I was constantly provided with a diversion from the realities of life. I should have known it couldn't last.

As the second year of our marriage unfolded, I began to question my decision to leave the States. While the dramatic changes I had brought into my life had dulled my awareness to the signals from my body, when the newness wore off, it seemed to recall my illness with a vengeance, and there were times I was unable to accomplish the simplest of tasks. Once again I was back in a doctor's office, this time a prominent Air Force physician's. His diagnosis was much more ominous than any I'd received before.

"Malignancy . . . immediate surgery." The words echoed from a long distance away. Though I heard him clearly, it was as if I'd been drugged. I recall little of what else he may have said.

They called Tom into the room. "I'm sorry honey," he said. "They're going to do everything they can. Don't be afraid. You'll get the best treatment."

I wasn't afraid. I just didn't quite accept it. Their words seemed directed toward someone else. Though I was only twenty-seven years old, maybe that was enough. Anyway, I had never feared death. At that moment I was enveloped in a protective cocoon that kept away the fear as well as my awareness of the seriousness of my situation.

I wasn't allowed to return home. Tom tried to console me. "They're going to send you to Germany for surgery. There's a plane leaving in three hours and they want us on it. They said they would get you whatever you need." He kept telling me about the wonderful doctors that would cure me.

It wasn't until we boarded the plane that I acknowledged what was happening. I still wasn't afraid, but I began to think about death. I didn't really care what the doctors were going to do. It didn't seem to matter. If I died, nothing would matter. I wouldn't have to deal with it.

I'm sure most people assumed I was depressed, and maybe I was. I had been sick for three years. Whatever they suggested was okay with me. And I didn't care about the future. I might not have one.

The doctor at the military hospital in Germany confirmed what I had already accepted. "I believe in being up front with my patients," he said. "We'll do everything we can, but the cancer has done a lot of damage."

"If you think you can fix me, I'm willing to try. What are my odds?" I asked. "And if I do recover, will I have a normal life?"

"There are a lot of variables, but I'd say no better than thirty-five per cent. We'll operate in the morning. After the surgery, we can discuss the future. Now you need to get your affairs in order." He confirmed his statement by calling in a stenographer for me to dictate my last will and testament.

Three days later I awoke in incredible pain. There was no one in the room, and I looked around, surprised to be alive. I had taken the first step at beating the odds. Maybe I would make it after all. I began to think about the ways I might change my life. I had hardly considered such an alternative.

Less than a month later I returned to Iran. My American and Iranian friends had arranged a homecoming, a celebration of my new life. I was thankful to have survived.

In the months that followed, life in Iran became more difficult, sometimes frightening. Terrorist bombings took place with increasing frequency, and it was no longer safe to go into the market. The government was rapidly losing control over a country I'd once found so wonderful. Of course, part of what I liked had been its westernization, something many of the locals detested.

The declining political situation had me practically confined to our apartment, and I became fearful when strangers appeared on the street below. When Tom announced his reassignment to Colorado, I was elated.

Shortly after we moved, the Iranian government collapsed into chaos. I was glad that I'd not been there to see it, and I feared for what might happen to our Iranian friends. But I had problems of my own to deal with, a marriage that had become as unstable as the political situation I had left behind. Lacking the foundation upon which our marriage should have been built, we began to realize that our differences were much more serious than we had previously admitted. Tom and I had come together with a hope for what we wanted our life to be, not for anything substantial that had existed.

Our expectations had been unrealistic, but we struggled through two more years before agreeing to divorce. I would make a new home somewhere far away and begin a new life. Maybe I would finally get it right.

Making a fresh start turned out to be more difficult than just moving to a new city. I lived in several different states, but it was always the same. They didn't feel like home. It took me four years to realize where I was supposed to be. My life journey had begun in the hills of north Georgia, and that's where I needed to return.

Once I made the move, everything seemed better, but I would spend several more years lost, in search of my true identity. During that time I avoided focusing upon my problems by working as much as possible. It wasn't necessarily a conscious effort on my part, but I'm sure a part of me was determined to keep my mind occupied. Most of the time I worked two jobs, sometimes three.

I believe my death experience was used to get my attention, to shake me out of the stupor in which I'd been living. It was obviously an extreme measure, but I'm convinced I would never have discovered my path without it.

Another powerful catalyst for my awakening was meeting my present and wonderful husband, Mike. We met on the job, both working for the same company, and it was love at first sight. Once I experienced it, I understood why my other relationships had never worked out. Mike and I had immediately recognized that we were making the right choice, and we were married in less than a year.

The next three years were incredible. Everything seemed as I had always dreamed it would be. Although my life-view was still pretty immature, I was deeply in love and gave little thought to the superficial way I was living. I also continued working as much as sixty hours a week, but my new husband and I made the best of the limited time we could be together. What I couldn't know was that I was on a collision course with myself where I would discover how much there was for me to learn about both love and life. I needed help, needed to change my direction. The time had come for the angels to intervene.

CHAPTER 4

Transformation

The death experience had blindsided me. I'd never been one to examine the spiritual side of life and had never seriously questioned my purpose, but the visits with the angels and the young woman in the cave had changed all that. Even though I didn't understand, I couldn't ignore what was happening. It meant something. It had to.

As the months passed I tried to find meaning, but I'd come no closer to understanding than when it had happened. It just didn't make sense. I had hoped that time might help me gain clarity, but each passing week only brought more questions.

Though I had a great relationship with my new husband, Mike, I felt I couldn't tell him what had happened. It was impossible to describe the experiences without sounding crazy, and I didn't know how he might react. What if he didn't believe me, and if he did, would he still feel the same about me?

I was filled with questions. What had caused the experiences? Had I overlooked the obvious? In the quiet just before dawn I often prayed for guidance. If I couldn't find the answers on my own, maybe God would help.

The unusual stillness as the world awakens is a great time for reflection. Although I've never considered myself a morning person, the birth of a new day brings a sense of internal awakening, pushing the past into memory and offering encouragement for the future. I used that time to search for answers.

In the silence I asked for understanding, but none came. I was so confused I couldn't sort through it all. I had thought that going back to work might help. If I couldn't explain what I'd experienced, at least I might be able to put it out of my mind. A few weeks after returning, however, I realized it had only made matters worse.

I had once been attracted to the world of big business and had worked hard to prove myself worthy of my position and future positions I hoped would come. The company where I was employed provided cleaning services to major corporate clients. The work was both demanding and stressful, an environment I had previously enjoyed. When they had offered a major promotion, I was thrilled; moving up the corporate ladder was exactly what I'd wanted. Though I knew I'd been selected for a reason, that one of the men had refused the same job, I was flattered they had thought me qualified, and determined to show everyone I could do it.

One of my responsibilities—the reason most couldn't stomach the job—was that I had to fire all those who didn't meet the company's performance standards. My aggressive, no-nonsense approach soon earned me the nickname, "terminator," a title I wore like a badge, justifying each firing by convincing myself that the lazy or incompetent only hurt those who remained. My heart was quickly hardened to the pitiful stories I heard, and I never hesitated from executing my duties.

Though I was small, little more than five feet, I was strong, both physically and emotionally and feared by many of my coworkers. I enjoyed the sense of power I felt. Workers lowered their heads and stepped aside when I approached, and I once overheard the comment: "I wouldn't want to meet her in a dark alley."

I look back with embarrassment and shame at my lack of compassion. It's difficult to understand how I could have ever been such a bully, so ego-centered. Even though my experiences may have been a necessary part of my growth, I shudder when I realize what a nasty person I had been.

Something about the death experience had changed me, and once I did return to work, I found it more difficult to focus on my job than I had anticipated. I'd only been back for three days when I had my first visit to the cave, and although I was shaken, the event was only the beginning of a bizarre series of things to come. In the weeks that followed, my subterranean journeys began to occur with increasing frequency. Soon they were coming every day and always in the same manner.

Sitting with my morning coffee, I would be whisked into another dimension. I began to anticipate the experiences and the calming, almost narcotic, effect they had. The journeys themselves were pleasurable, though I suffered afterwards from fears and worries about what had caused them. As each day unfolded, I could see myself changing in ways I had never before thought possible.

I could no longer ignore the impact my decisions had on the lives of others, and my co-workers noticed the dramatic shift in my personality. Their reactions made me feel like an outsider. A kinder, gentler self had surfaced, and I began to resist the demands and pressures from my superiors. I couldn't blind myself to the feelings of those I was expected to fire. I was connected to them, wanted to understand them, and help with their problems.

There was also an unusual, but welcomed, benefit to my transformation. My body seemed to undergo a noticeable change in appearance. Although I couldn't see it, those who had hardly noticed me before offered compliments about the new me, and I received a number of questions about what I had changed. "Was I on a diet, an exercise plan? Had I colored or cut my hair?"

I had done none of those things and was not consciously doing anything different. Although I had lost a few pounds, I felt I looked the same.

However, there was something much more unusual than a mere change in appearance. My senses had grown intensely acute, and I noticed things I had never before acknowledged. Driving to work I marveled at the beauty that surrounded me—giant oak trees, their branches lifted toward heaven, the majestic mountain range that stood only a few miles north of my home, and the playful antics of squirrels racing to stock their pantry for winter. Flocks of geese soaring overhead hypnotized me with their grace and symmetry. The simplest of things, such as ants marching across the lawn, could capture my attention and cause me to forget whatever errand I might have been on.

It may seem trivial, but I felt a connection with every creature I encountered, whether insect, animal, or human. I was also conscious of the energy of inanimate objects, especially stones. Much more than just an awareness of things I had once ignored, more than just an improvement in my sight or hearing, I received information through some unknown ability, knowledge of things I should have no way of knowing.

My new insights didn't bring acceptance, however, they only served to widen the separation between me and my fellow workers. I often wondered if my bizarre experiences were punishment for past deeds. Desperate faces of those I had fired sometimes haunted me when I lay in bed at night. Perhaps my callousness and insensitivity had caught up with me; and my co-workers seemed to sense my loss of power. I sometimes overheard their conversations and received raised eyebrows as they puzzled over my strange behavior.

The appearance of my softer side was only a slight curiosity; however, the change that was most significant was my ability to tap into some master source of knowledge. I could see into events and actions with awareness of what had motivated the action. I would know what was in someone's heart, regardless of what they said, and pictures sometimes appeared in my mind of unfolding events, even though I was not present at the time they occurred. At first I shared a few of those insights, but as it became obvious that the information was far beyond intuition, I kept them to myself.

During that time a girlfriend and I took a weekend trip to the mountains. With lots of time for "girl-talk," I described some personal events from her past that I had seen in a vision. She was shocked that I knew things she had never shared with anyone. "You really do have the power," she said. "But what you're doing isn't normal, and it's none of your business. I don't like it."

For the remainder of that weekend we spoke only a few times. She was angry that I had seen into her personal life and was afraid of the ability that had allowed me to do it. After we returned home she refused to return my phone calls. I hadn't meant to frighten or embarrass her. I hoped she could help me understand what was happening to me.

An event at work, however, showed how some of my insights could be helpful. When an expensive commercial vacuum disappeared from our office storeroom, I was shown a vision of where it was. A moving picture formed in my mind, allowing me to see the entire episode replayed as it had occurred. I watched as one of our employees waited for his co-workers to leave, then grabbed the equipment and hurriedly stashed it away until it would be safe to take out of the building. In my mind I followed him into a seldom used area of the basement where he hid his bounty under an empty carton. I was disturbed by what I had seen, but had no way of knowing if my vision were true. However, I was certain I wasn't daydreaming. Everything was so real, so clear. I felt I had seen what really happened.

I sat at my desk all afternoon trying to decide what to do. A part of me didn't want confirmation. When I could no longer resist, I called my boss, Jim, and told him I knew who had taken the equipment and where it was hidden. I asked him to accompany me to the basement. As we walked down the stairs, he quizzed me about how I could know who the culprit was. I responded that it was just a hunch, a feeling that had come to me that morning. I wasn't about to describe my vision or the recent events that caused me to believe it might be true.

Jim trusted me, and though he didn't seem completely satisfied with my explanation, he was curious enough to indulge me. What he didn't know was that I was more bewildered than he was. I didn't understand how or why the information had come to me, and I wasn't sure what I was doing. I was pulled by an unseen force, and had to know if what I'd seen was accurate.

We entered the basement and walked down a long corridor lined with large boxes, all similar to the one I had seen in my vision. I passed several of them before coming to an abrupt halt. "Here," I said, pointing to one of the boxes. I lifted it up. When I set it aside, hidden underneath was the stolen vacuum just as I had pictured.

Jim looked at me with astonishment. "Thanks," he said. "I guess you know what to do." He walked away mumbling something about my psychic powers. The reputation I'd once held was being replaced by one less malicious, but more unusual and more threatening to some, and I was more mystified than anyone.

I called the suspected employee into my office and told him we had found the vacuum. His look of surprise and stammered explanation confirmed what I already knew. I was convinced that his termination was justified. Those that followed were not so easy.

After several uncomfortable months I turned in my resignation. The corporate world no longer held an attraction. Instead, I was repulsed by the dishonesty and lack of compassion that seemed an inherent part of business. I couldn't live what I considered a lie. I wasn't sure what I would do, but I would never again be the person once known as "the terminator." My personality, the way I viewed everything around me, had been turned upside down, and the changes gnawed at my soul. Torn from the life I once enjoyed, I felt like a wanderer, pausing before a fork in the road. The path I was choosing led into the unknown. Was I making the right choice? I prayed that it would lead me out of the darkness.

CHAPTER 5

Divine Intervention or Insanity?

In the weeks just prior to my resignation, my daily visits to the cave had grown longer and more intense. Each morning there were new experiences and new revelations. It was good that my work didn't begin early, for some of my excursions lasted more than an hour, and the more time I spent underground, the more pleasurable the visits became. Although I was concerned for my sanity, I looked forward to my visits with Maya, and developed a routine that encouraged our subterranean encounters. Her lessons and gentle way of teaching nourished me. She embodied the essence of everything I needed—compassion, love, and patience—unbelievable patience.

As I think back to that time, I don't believe either of us ever uttered a sound, but we communicated with a clarity that transcended words. I received her thoughts just as clearly as if she were speaking, and she seemed to receive mine the same. I never questioned how such communication was possible; in her dimension it seemed perfectly normal.

Maya seemed to enjoy her role as my teacher, and I tried to be a good student. She helped me forget my problems, and at times, I was able to bring some of the comforting feelings back into my other world. I relished the time we spent together.

Each day I was instructed in new and wonderful ways of healing and taught how to share my knowledge with others. She showed me how I could draw energy from the earth, water, and stones. Stone power, she said, connected us with our earth mother. Wearing or carrying them helped to maintain that connection.

"There was once a time when all acknowledged their relationship to our precious and beautiful earth, but that time has been forgotten." She grasped a brilliant crystal that hung from her neck. "This stone draws energy from those that light our path." She pointed to the sparkling crystals in the cave's wall. "I call upon it to enlighten my mind."

She explained how earth or stone energy could be used to send healing and comfort to others. I could energize myself by walking outdoors barefoot. Wearing shoes obstructed the flow of energy. "There is more power in our Earth mother than we can possibly know," she said. "If we will only open ourselves, she will eagerly share it with us.

"Stones hold great strength, and are filled with wisdom. We know them as the record keepers of earth."

Maya suggested I use stones in my initial healing efforts, for their energy is easiest to direct. By holding a stone near an injury I could send healing rays into a person. It wasn't even necessary for me to understand how it worked.

"If you ask for Spirit's guidance, you will not harm a person. You will be shown how and where to place the stone. In future times you will learn to use your hands, pulling in energy from the Universe and transferring it to the person you are healing."

I could send energy, she said, even though the person might not be aware I was doing it. "Sometimes a gentle touch on the shoulder is all that is necessary to send healing. If the person is ready to be healed, and if that is their agreement with Spirit, it will be done. But never forget that you are only the instrument; you do not make the choice for another."

She taught me how I could also use color, sound, or one of the elements. Spirit would guide me.

"My favorites are the stones," she said. She held out a small woven basket. "The way to choose one is to first hold it and feel its energy. Ask if it can help you in your work. If it says yes, and you feel that its energy is strong, Spirit will direct you how to use it."

I took the basket. Inside were a dozen or more stones of different colors, shapes, and sizes. There were brilliant crystals about three inches long and several small smooth stones that ranged in color from shiny black to light gray. "Choose one," she said.

I reached inside.

"Wait. First, you must close your eyes. Do not be guided by appearance. Feel their energy, their power. They may feel cold or warm. Listen to your inner voice. Choose the one that speaks to you."

I moved my hand around the basket, allowing my fingers to touch each surface. I lifted them, one by one, and held them in my palm. There was a difference! It was amazing. A couple felt so cold I held them only seconds before returning them to the basket. It was obvious they weren't right. Some of the others felt warm and comfortable, but I eventually dropped them too. Then I understood what she meant. One of the stones drew me like a magnet and I pulled it out and held it against my chest.

When I opened my eyes, Maya was smiling. "You listened. You let Spirit and the voice of the stone speak to your heart."

I looked down to my palm. A sparkling amethyst glistened with an inner brilliance. As I rubbed its surface, my fingertips tingled as if with an electrical charge.

"Take it with you. You will use it and others to help you bring healing into your world. It is a gift from the earth."

Later, I awoke still sitting in my chair. Mentally I felt great, but my body was exhausted. I sat there for more than an hour thinking about what had happened, the lessons I'd received. It all seemed so real, yet I knew it couldn't be. I was sure there was an explanation I had not considered. I hoped it wasn't an indication of something terribly wrong with me.

When I stood up, I looked to the floor. There between my feet was the beautiful amethyst Maya had given me! I picked it up and squeezed it in my palm. I didn't know how it could have appeared, but I was thankful it had come. Perhaps I was crazy, but the stone gave me a feeling of stability. I loved it.

During the time I worked with her, there were other experiences that pointed to the unusual nature of the path I had begun to follow. I saw things in my mind, had knowledge of things to come, and became aware of another dimension that surrounds us. That other dimension, I understood, is a reflection of the part we can see, but it holds much more information. Those who can see it can learn how to predict the future and how to detect what is true on this plane.

The unusual energy surrounding me also affected my husband, Mike. He too sometimes experienced things others would consider supernatural. Once he came home and observed what he described as strange balls of blue light circling around the room. When he turned on the lamp, the lights remained for a moment, then gradually faded away.

Other experiences happened when we were together, such as hearing inexplicable noises and voices that came out of nowhere. Lights and appliances would flicker on and off, and though we couldn't ignore the strange phenomena, we seldom discussed them. I made jokes and laughingly referred to the gremlins that had infested our house. I wanted to know what Mike thought of it, but I didn't ask out of fear he might connect it with me.

There were also powerful events I experienced alone. Those I never mentioned. Once, after falling asleep on the sofa, I awoke to the sound of panting, similar to that of a dog, and very close. When I opened my eyes, I looked directly into the face of a mountain lion. I could feel its breath, see its eyes staring into mine. As soon as I raised up, the creature vanished.

Sure I was afraid, but not of the things I saw. I knew they weren't real. They were just more of my strange visions. I was frightened because they represented the part of me that was beyond my control, and I couldn't understand why I had to experience them.

One of my more unusual visitors was a Confederate soldier in full uniform who appeared in my living room. At the time, I lived in an area rich in Civil War history. There had been a great battle only a few miles from my home, and thousands of soldiers on both sides had died. I had visited the local museum and seen the displays. I was sure the young man who appeared to me was one of those who had died there.

I saw him clearly, a face smeared with blood and dirt, and hardly more than twenty years old—a child gone to war. His arms held a musket, and a tattered jacket hung loosely on his gaunt frame. I knew he was from another reality, for I could also see through him to the room beyond. He looked at me with eyes that expressed great sadness, yet something about his appearance told me there was nothing to fear. He was trapped in an unknown dimension, frightened and confused, and I felt I had to help him.

A prayer formed in my mind. "Go to the light." The words came easily. As soon as they were spoken, the room lit up as if by a lightning flash and the soldier vanished, never to return.

Although I had not been frightened by the encounter, I still feared for what was happening to me. If Mike or others knew about my experiences I might be more than ostracized. They might want to put me in an institution. How could I expect anyone to understand and accept something so bizarre?

Sometimes after having one of the visions, I would remember the strange events from my childhood—the dreams that came true. I wondered if there might be a connection. I prayed for guidance, hoping the God I had ignored during the first half of my life would take pity on me and keep me from going insane. I wanted to know the meaning of what had happened—if there was one. If not, I wanted to be able to forget everything and get on with my life.

My recovery from the death experience caused me to feel I'd cheated fate. What had brought me back? Had the angels really intervened? If so, why? I thought back to other times I had been spared from death.

In my late teens I seriously contemplated suicide, made plans for how I would do it. When I was ready, a commanding voice stopped me cold. "No," it said. The voice was so loud and compelling that

I changed my mind. Maybe someone did care, even if it wasn't someone I could see.

There was also a time I fell asleep at the wheel, driving home from a late-night party. I had not been drinking, but was completely oblivious to everything that happened, including leaving the pavement—evidenced by heavy mud splatters all down the side of my car. Something had guided me safely for several miles, and I had no memory of how I had managed to get home.

Such experiences made me feel as if I had been spared for a reason. What else could explain it? I could count at least four occasions my life seemed to have been saved, times when voices, visions, and unforgettable visits with angels had delivered me from death. As I put them all together, they pointed to the fact that my life had been protected by a force I couldn't understand. There had to be something other than mere coincidence. For me the evidence seemed overwhelming.

I puzzled over why I had been singled out. What made my life different from millions of others? Why was I worthy of divine intervention? I wasn't even religious. Religion had never been a significant part of my life.

My work with Maya provided a possible answer, but it seemed so far-fetched I hardly considered it. And the questions it raised only increased my confusion and concern for my sanity. I continually struggled to separate illusion from reality.

If I wasn't crazy, what was happening to me? Had I suffered a stroke? Was there some chemical imbalance in my brain that caused me to see and feel things that weren't there? Whatever was going on, the encounters themselves usually left me with a good feeling, and the healing lessons were captivating. I enjoyed that part, eager to learn more, even though I didn't think of myself as a healer. I felt sure I'd one day discover that my experiences had only been dreams; the things I'd seen couldn't have been real. My understanding was about to make an abrupt turn.

CHAPTER 6

Exploring the Cave

The underground journeys continued for nearly a year, and during that time I made notes of some of the more unusual occurrences. I wouldn't begin to document the events in detail until months later when I realized the importance of what had happened.

No longer disturbed by the subterranean environment, I grew more interested in the surroundings. The cave was enormous, a huge cavern with connecting tunnels that extended for miles. Much of it seemed to have been designated for specific purposes, and in one area I saw what appeared to be sleeping quarters cut into the walls.

Although my visits with Maya were usually in the same area, on occasion she had taken me into other parts, much of which appeared to be unexplored. I remember passing a couple of places with no lighting, dark recesses where tunnels extended into the blackness. Maya's description made them sound even more mysterious. "No one is allowed to enter here. There is danger that we do not speak of."

The inhabited areas appeared to be the complete living quarters for an entire group of people. Strangely, I saw few of them during all of my visits. According to Maya there were many more as well as other healers who worked in different parts of the cave, but I never saw any of them either. Those adults I saw appeared to be in their twenties or thirties. I rarely encountered anyone that looked over fifty.

Something I found most intriguing was the cave's lighting which came from three distinct sources. Tiny crystals embedded in the walls projected a dim glow that made it possible to see, but little more. There were also a few scattered fires that burned continuously in those areas where the healings took place, and a dozen or more domed shafts that extended up through the roof, bringing in light from above.

The light shafts served as greenhouses with plant ledges spaced along their walls. The plants grown there had thick leaves which, when pressed, produced a liquid that was mixed with water and consumed by the cave's inhabitants. I assumed the mixture provided some sort of nutritional benefit.

I saw a few pools of water, but Maya said it wasn't safe to drink. An elaborate purification system was used to remove the contaminates, and the purified water was stored in areas where the people could drink whenever they wanted. However, they seemed to need little as I rarely saw anyone drinking, and when they did, it consisted of taking in only a few drops of water, sometimes mixed with leaf juice. I never saw anyone eating solid food.

The unusual nature of the underground environment became more evident with each visit. In all my time there I encountered no more than twenty of the cave's inhabitants, though I'd been told there were hundreds more. Strangely, those I saw seemed oblivious to my presence. They never communicated with me, and the few times they interacted with Maya, they ignored me altogether.

There was only one time I ever felt that anyone other than Maya knew I was there. During my first visit, when the young girl was being healed, it appeared that she had seen me. After her healing she left with the two adults I had seen standing nearby. When she was walking away, she had turned to me and smiled. The others never looked back.

Maya sometimes spoke of a Council of Elders, the decision makers for the group. They had taught her the ways of healing, she said, but I never knew which ones they were. She seemed to accept the elders as superior to everyone else, having knowledge of things the others lacked. They knew about the outside world, although it wasn't clear whether or not they had actually been there. Maya described what they had told her about the land above.

"In times past the world was green—green with lots of leaves," she said. "It would have been wonderful." The way she described it gave me a sense she longed to see it. But she had never been outside, she said; to go there was forbidden. There was a fear that poisonous conditions existed, and all the exits from the cave were closed.

Although I wondered how long the people had been in the cave, I never asked. The experience had kept me somewhat in awe, and I ignored what seemed to be insignificant questions.

When I asked about the world above, it seemed to rekindle Maya's interest. She described what she had been told and stared blankly ahead as if trying to experience it in her mind. She spoke of how wonderful it would be to live in such a place, and at some point she told me she would explore it for herself. "It is time," she said.

Although I was concerned about the poisoned atmosphere, I immediately answered, "I'll go with you." It seemed natural to offer my help, and a few days later I followed her into a secluded area where one of the light shafts was no longer used. A heavy wooden frame had been constructed around the opening and thick boards slipped inside to create a barrier.

Maya slid several of the boards aside and pulled her slender body through the narrow opening. There was barely enough room for the two of us, but I quickly followed, squeezing into the tiny space. When we were both inside, she sealed the shaft once more.

The old plant ledges were like steps alternating from side to side, and we carefully pulled ourselves up. The shaft must have been sealed for many years for it smelled of stale, moldy dirt and rotting wood.

Climbing upward was much more difficult than I had imagined, and our progress was painstakingly slow. Because she was above me, her body blocked most of the light, and I had to feel my way along.

When she finally reached the top, she slowly pushed the domed covering open. A rush of air whooshed past, and for a moment I held my breath, afraid to inhale. When I could hold it no longer, I gasped and filled my lungs to capacity. The air smelled fresh and clean, a dramatic change from that of the cave.

"Come," Maya said. She disappeared over the side of the dome.

Bright light streamed into the shaft, temporarily blinding me, and I paused for a moment, allowing my eyes adjust. I resumed my climb when I heard her voice. "Do not be afraid. There are new lessons for you in this place."

I inched forward, clawing into the dirt walls. When I reached the top I pulled myself out of the shaft and looked around. Maya was standing about twenty feet away. She gave an approving nod and smiled.

The place was a paradise. There was dense vegetation everywhere. It reminded me of rainforest pictures I'd seen. Everything was deep green. As much as the beauty, though, I was struck by the intense silence. There were no birds, no animals, and no people.

Maya came over and pushed the dome back into place and stood silently for several minutes. I wondered if she might be having second thoughts. After a couple of minutes she led me through a small opening in the thick growth as if she knew where she was going. We had walked for about ten minutes when we came upon a stream. I remember looking into the water, sparkling as the light played on its surface. Maya looked at it too, and I felt she wanted to taste it, but she didn't. Something told me it was safe, and I cupped my hands and took a few sips. It was cool and refreshing.

A few minutes later we left the stream and started up a steep embankment. Our climb was slow and difficult as the lush canopy overhead blocked out most of the light. Several times I slipped and fell. Maya waited patiently, providing help when I needed it.

We had climbed for about ten minutes when we reached a plateau where the forest opened up. Ahead I heard a loud rushing noise. Walking in the direction of the sound, we came into a valley where several streams converged, plummeting from the surrounding hillsides. We paused and stared, practically encircled by a dozen or more beautiful waterfalls. The view was spectacular.

Maya pointed to a large rock. "We will learn from the spirit of the waters," she said. And we sat quietly, the roar of the falls creating a din that was almost hypnotic. A couple of times I saw her nod as if someone had spoken, but all I heard was the crashing of the water onto the rocks. She seemed fascinated by her surroundings, studying her environment with the keen interest of a scientist making a new discovery. I watched as she examined some of the small stones at her feet. I was sure she was communicating with them in the same way she did with me.

Off to our left a huge tree towered over the forest, its silhouette painting a dark shadow against a cloudless sky, more purple than blue. The place seemed familiar, yet I knew it was not from my world. I felt we were the only ones there.

That first visit outside the cave ended as we relaxed, enjoying the sound and beauty of the water. I was returned to my home feeling more at peace than I had in months.

In my later visits Maya taught me about the plants that grew near the falls. She pointed out those that were edible and those with medicinal properties. As she described them, she lovingly stroked each one, spoke to them, and gave a blessing to Spirit for providing them for our food and healing needs.

"Yes, Nature is our ally," she said. "And though the plants are here for our use, they too have life. They are to be respected and treated with love. If you must use one, first ask its permission and ask for a blessing for both you and it. Pray that Spirit will use the plant's energy to feed you or to cure your illness. Never harm a plant without cause, for to do so is to harm yourself."

Maya taught me how to listen to Nature, to the voice of the wind—sometimes gentle, sometimes fearsome. She showed me how to hear the voice within a frolicking stream as it tumbled over the rocks, to hear the trees, their mighty chorus echoing throughout the forest. "There is beautiful music here if you will listen," she said. And the melody I heard was more powerful, more majestic, and more harmonious than any I'd heard in my other life. It reminded me of my first visit with the angels.

Learning to hear the voices was only the first step. I could speak with the stones, with trees, the rushing waters of a river, and could listen for answers to my innermost questions. The elements of Nature bring energy into our bodies and minds. When we acknowledge our connection, we access an unlimited source that can help us heal ourselves and others.

As I try to convey what I learned and experienced, I struggle with the inability to express it all. It is impossible to put into words the sensations and emotions I felt, the knowledge I received. I saw the simplicity of life and understood how we are the ones who create an illusion of complexity. We bring the turmoil into our lives. Life is pure and perfect. The imperfection we see comes from the illusion and blinds us to the eternal.

My visits with Maya continued for two more months, but after our exit from the cave we always met at the waterfall. I would not return to her underground world again. When I had been with her, I never questioned the unusual nature of our surroundings, nor did I ask her to explain the circumstance of our meeting—in her presence everything seemed to be as it should. I found more comfort there than in what I considered my real world.

Each time I returned to that other reality, however, I always looked back in confusion. How could I explain such bizarre experiences? Where did the visions come from? Were they a view from the past? People dressed in animal skins and working before fires seemed to make it so.

There were times I wondered if my visions had come from an unknown future, a foreboding of a great cataclysmic event? I wasn't sure, and I never received an answer.

What I questioned most was what made the visions appear. More than once I voiced to myself what I really felt. "You're crazy,"

I would say. "One of these days the little men in white coats will come to get you."

Whether or not my visions came from some distant past or foretell a disastrous future is unimportant. The setting provided an opportunity for me to learn from those I consider to be masters—masters in the healing arts as well as beings spiritually advanced far beyond me.

My final visit with Maya was perhaps the most dramatic. "Tell me," I asked. "Who are you—the real you?"

"You know who I am," she said.

"Show me," I pleaded. "I have to know."

"You already know. Acknowledge the awareness that is within." As she spoke, her robe fell to the ground and her body melted away. There was nothing but light, pure light, so bright I lowered my head to shield my face.

I heard her voice, "Now you will have the gift you were promised in the light."

Her words sparked a memory from months before—the day I had died. For some reason I had not connected her with the light beings that had left me with the promise I would one day, "Teach and heal."

Memories of things they had shown me stirred within and waves of emotion swept over me. It wasn't that I was sad, for I had awakened to a world I never knew existed. I was filled with a sense of purpose, of self-worth, and an overwhelming awareness of the loving presence that would be with me always.

When I looked up, Maya was gone. Her robe lay on the ground before me. I picked it up and held it close, squeezing hard as if it might bring her back. Her wonderful lessons had bound us together for nine months; I desperately wanted just one more minute.

Much more than a fascinating and informative teacher, Maya was an angel sent by a loving God to help get my life back on course. The things she had taught had transformed me in ways I had only begun to see. I had learned about healing, but more importantly, I had learned how to heal myself, a necessary first step to helping others. Through her I had caught a glimpse of the real me, the part that is connected with all else, the part connected to God.

I never again visited the cave, never returned to the waterfall, but that wasn't the end of my journey. It was the beginning of a wondrous adventure of healing, learning, and sharing. My training had ended; the time for action had begun.

CHAPTER 7

Integrating the Experiences

With the most intense portion of my instruction ended and a new phase beginning, there was much to be excited about. However, as I thought about the previous months, I could imagine how others would be skeptical, perhaps even afraid, of the new life that was unfolding for me. What would I tell people about my experiences? How could I describe Maya, the angels, the cave? Who would believe me if I tried? I was especially concerned about how Mike would react. We were approaching our fourth year together, yet I had never discussed any of my paranormal experiences.

It wasn't so much that I didn't want to share what had happened to me or that I doubted his commitment. I knew he loved me, but I was afraid. Mother had loved me too, but when I told her about my special dreams, she had threatened to send me away.

When I finally found the courage to tell Mike, I had him make a promise. Though I loved him dearly and trusted him completely, I was terrified of his reaction.

"I need your help," I began. "I think I might be losing my mind. Promise me you won't send me away."

"Don't worry," he laughed. "You're not going anywhere." But he had no idea what I was about to say, or the seriousness of my concerns.

I began my story, starting with the death experience. I described how I'd floated above my body, how I'd seen him that morning, described his expression as he drove my car following the ambulance.

He raised his hand and interrupted. "You're serious," he said. "How did you know I drove your car?" His face contorted and he wrinkled his brow. "You know I don't like driving it. How did you know?"

"I saw you," I repeated. Mike had always preferred his pickup truck and refused to take my car even for errands, though it sometimes meant moving it when it blocked his truck.

"I'm not sure why I drove the car," he said. "I didn't even think about it until later, and there was no reason to mention it."

He knew I shouldn't have known what he had driven that morning. After all, I was unconscious when they wheeled me out of the house. He wrapped me in his big arms and gave me a hug. "Tell me the rest," he said. He slid back into his chair. His face was turned towards me, his eyes staring into mine, but I could see his thoughts were somewhere else. "Go ahead," he said. He patted my hands. For the next hour I recounted the events of the previous months.

Mike listened without interruption until I had finished my story. Afterwards he sat quietly for a couple of minutes while I twitched in my chair, nervous about his response.

Finally, he looked at me and smiled. "It sounds wonderful. I'm sorry you were afraid to share it with me."

"You don't think I'm crazy?"

"I think you may have received a very special gift," he said. "This weekend we'll go into Atlanta. There are some bookstores where we can find some information to help explain what you experienced. Don't worry. You're not crazy. I've always known you were pretty special. Now I just think you're more special."

His response lifted an enormous weight from my shoulders. He was more loving and understanding than I could have imagined and seemed genuinely interested in learning about what had happened. In the coming weeks he would take me to metaphysical bookstores and study centers so we could discover more about the experiences.

Mike and I grew closer than ever as we tried to unravel the meaning behind my death experience and the healing lessons I wanted to use to help others. The supernatural world had never interested me and I knew almost nothing about it; but Mike seemed to know everything. His insatiable appetite for knowledge had led him to read dozens of metaphysical books years earlier. He was familiar with books, authors, and areas of study I had never heard of, and his understanding of near death experiences—I prefer to call mine a death experience for I'm convinced I died—and journeys out of the body helped us to find the information we needed. Having him at my side was a great relief, and I relied on him to guide me in the right direction.

Our search led us to some remarkable people who helped me understand the trauma my psyche had undergone. I gained confidence in myself and the knowledge I had received and began to share Maya's lessons with those I felt wanted to know. My death experience and the time spent with my guides were gifts that would allow me to help others, and I was eager to do so.

Although I didn't understand it at the time, I seemed to attract those to me who needed my help. There were times when I would be attending presentations or workshops and would be approached by complete strangers who would ask me to give advice about health or relationship problems. They seemed to sense I could see into their lives, and I was regularly called upon for spiritual guidance. Though I didn't feel competent to act as anyone's spiritual advisor—I needed more guidance than most—I felt an obligation to use the talents Spirit had provided.

Many times I wouldn't know if my advice had been helpful because I might never see the person again, but those times when I could see how I had helped provided additional confirmation that the messages were true. The ones that were most convincing were the times I would receive information about a person the moment we would meet.

After months of study and after being advised by my guides to become more active in trying to reach others, I asked them to show me what to do. When a local metaphysical center advertised for a volunteer receptionist, I interpreted that to be a door opening for me. I had no idea what to expect from the job, but I thought working there might provide some sort of connection that would help me to use what I had learned. I felt confident Spirit was guiding me.

A few days later I drove to the store to meet the owners, two women I had met earlier in my search. The pair greeted me at the door. "I can feel your energy," one said. "I felt it the day you called."

Once inside they asked me to follow them to a small room where we sat at a table. With hands outstretched they faced me and smiled.

Something told me to grasp their hands, and I gazed into their eyes. "I'm not sure how much I can help," I said. "But, I'm ready to try." I was referring to my volunteer duties.

Several minutes later I shook my head. "I'm sorry. I feel as though I fell asleep." The two women were sobbing.

"That's incredible," one said. "You know things about us we've never shared with anyone. When I spoke with you on the phone, I knew you were special. You have the gift."

I was dazed, unsure of what had happened or what I had said.

"We would love to have you work here. We have many clients who would benefit from your abilities."

I was bewildered. "I'll just be answering the phone, won't I?"

"You'll do much more than that, I'm sure," one responded. "There are a lot of people you can help."

I had only been looking for more exposure to the metaphysical world, but I agreed, somewhat confused about what they expected me to do. I hoped I was making the right choice, that I hadn't misunderstood how Spirit was guiding me.

Soon after our meeting I began working at the center, performing receptionist duties and studying whenever I had an opportunity. I read several books about near-death experiences and participated in a number of workshops, but I failed to discover information about anyone with experiences similar to mine.

One Friday afternoon during an unusually busy period a man came to receive a psychic reading. All of the readers were occupied, and one of the owners asked me if I would read for the man. "You can do it," she said. "You have no idea of the ability you have."

I reluctantly agreed, unsure of what I was supposed to do. "Don't worry," she said, "Ask for guidance and you'll know what to do."

I led the man into one of the private areas and we sat down. He seemed much more confident than I was.

I asked for his hands—something I'd seen the other readers do—and closed my eyes. A prayer formed in my mind and I said it aloud, asking for guidance and that the man receive the information he needed. Almost immediately I went into a trance-like state. It was as if I fell asleep.

I wasn't aware of what messages came through for the man, and I had no desire to know. For me such communications were private—between the individual and God.

When I returned to normal consciousness, I was still holding his hands. "Wow! Thank you. I really needed to hear that," he said. I was glad he was pleased, but wondered what he had experienced.

It wasn't until many months later that I began to be aware of the information passing through me, and by that time I'd decided that my conscious awareness might be helpful.

At the center I was constantly surrounded by people who not only accepted my unusual abilities but who encouraged me to understand and develop them. One of my new friends taught me a meditation technique that, she said, would help me fulfill my mission.

Through meditation I learned how to be aware when my guides were speaking to me, and I received insights and messages I was sure came from another dimension. I suppose it's because of my Cherokee heritage that the guides who came to me were all Native American.

The first to come after Maya was Walks with Moon, a young healer who uses song or tones to assist me. I sometimes hear her clear voice when I'm performing a healing, but there are also times when her voice comes through me. I will begin singing in the ancient language without conscious effort on my part. But she doesn't sing with my voice. Mine is coarse and raspy, and I could never carry a tune. When she sings through me, it's clear and melodious, and her songs are enchanting. She gives the impression that she is a gentle soul, kind and loving, and filled with healing energy.

On the other extreme, I have two male guides who are strong and warrior-like. One Feather, my guardian, only comes when I am threatened or to confirm that a situation is safe. There have been times he has literally jumped between me and another person, holding up his spear. "Go!" he shouts. His voice lets me know there is danger, and I've never waited to discover the dangers he is protecting me from.

There is also Chief Dance in the Sun, who brings wisdom and who has guided me through some difficult situations. While I don't see him, others have, but I sometimes feel his hand on my right shoulder. He is a stern, no-nonsense guide who once whacked me on the head when I jokingly misspoke his name.

The guides only come when I need their help, and I'm sometimes unaware of the reason for their appearance. Though I don't always understand, I've learned to accept their coming and the gifts they bring.

I recall one instance, early in my work at the center, when I was helping register people who had come to attend a workshop. Seated at a table near the door I signed in participants as they arrived. When a young man came in and said he was waiting for a friend, I directed him to take a seat across the room, then returned my attention to the registration forms in front of me. Moments later I was startled by an abrupt movement, and I looked up from my desk. The young man leaped to his feet and stepped backward, his body pressed against the wall, a look of shock and fear on his face.

"Is something wrong?" I asked. He made no response but stared wide-eyed in my direction.

"Do you need help?" I asked.

The young man's mouth opened slowly and his face paled. "There's a . . . an Indian . . . an Indian standing next to you," he stammered.

A reflex action caused me to turn and look to my side. "Yes, there," he said.

Though I saw no one, I felt a firm hand on my shoulder. Chief Dance in the Sun had made another visit. I smiled. "It's okay. He's a friend, one of my guides."

The young man ran out of the room, glancing over his shoulder as he left. And though I was never quite sure why my guide had appeared, I remain grateful for having such powerful allies.

John, who helped me get these memories onto paper, had an unusual experience when we first began working on the book. He always brought a small tape recorder to supplement the notes he took during our meetings and called me one morning to report a strange voice on his tape that was neither of ours. He had heard it the evening before as he was reviewing our previous session.

After listening to the tape several times, he had given up, unable to understand what the voice was saying. I told him to bring it the next time he came and I would see if I could decipher whatever was there.

A few weeks later John returned and gave me the tape. We put it in the recorder and turned it on. I couldn't help but laugh when I heard it. The voice was that of One Feather. He was speaking in the ancient language; that's why John couldn't understand him. My guide was giving his approval for what we were doing and letting me know that I was safe.

How did the voice get there? Why had we not heard it during our conversation? Those are questions I cannot answer. I do know that my guides are always with me, providing help, encouragement, and protection. For that I am grateful.

CHAPTER 8

My Work as a Channel

My successful introduction into channeling led to more requests, and I was soon overwhelmed by those seeking my advice. Some of my new friends encouraged me to advertise in the local metaphysical paper in order to reach even greater numbers, but I resisted, uncomfortable with the idea of promoting myself in such a manner. I felt I would reach those who truly needed me, that we would somehow be guided to meet. There was no need for promotion. The work I was doing came from Spirit, and the power wasn't mine. I was only a means for its expression in this dimension. I didn't need publicity and didn't want to appear to take credit for something that was far beyond my abilities.

Most of the readings I did were those I considered to be normal, that is, people wanted to know about job or relationship issues or how to deal with specific problems. Some asked about their health or the health of friends and family, and the angels occasionally recommended dietary or lifestyle changes or gave information about methods for healing. While most of the sessions were routine, a few were quite unusual, both for me and for those who had come seeking help.

Late one evening as the shop was preparing to close, the owner asked if I could do a reading for a new customer. As soon as she asked, an uneasy feeling formed in the pit of my stomach, but I dismissed it, thinking it came from my eagerness to go home. I was still learning the need to pay attention to such sensations, and my willingness to help others overruled what I now know to be Divine guidance.

A couple of minutes later a middle-aged gentleman walked up and stood in the doorway. "You the psychic?" he asked. Something about his eyes gave me an immediate chill.

"I do readings," I stammered. "Have a seat." Unaccustomed to the feelings I was receiving, I wasn't sure what to do next, but I didn't have to make that decision. My guides came to my rescue.

Before the man could take a seat, One Feather appeared between the two of us. His spear was raised high. "Go now," he shouted.

I didn't need to know more. I stood and walked to the front of the store, pausing at the front long enough to ask one of the assistants to tell the man I could not do his reading. With that I literally ran out the door and across the parking lot to my car.

I don't believe the man intended to harm me, but I'm not sure what might have happened if I had done his reading. He seemed to be surrounded by a terribly negative energy, and I felt there was no way I could help him. I don't think he was ready to be helped.

Whatever may have occurred, I'm convinced that my guides are aware of situations that are not visible to me, and I know to trust them when they speak. I have to believe that their guidance is in my best interest.

My connection with the spirit world occasionally produces strange and unusual events, and I've grown accustomed to the reactions of those who may not be aware of the visions I receive. There are times, however, when others have seen the results of my relationship with the guides.

Once, after a lady had asked me to give her a reading, she reached into her purse and produced a tape recorder. "Do you mind if I tape this?" she asked.

"No," I responded, "but you may want to make notes also. Others have tried to tape the sessions and have reported that their tapes came out garbled and filled with noise." At the time I was unsure what the problem might be, thinking it might relate to electrical interference or the fluorescent lighting.

The session lasted about thirty minutes and nothing unusual occurred. However, the lady called several days later and seemed quite upset. "I don't understand it," she said. "I used a brand new tape."

"Is there a problem?" I asked.

"Yes, it's strange. Every question I asked you is clearly recorded on the tape, but where your response should be, it's blank. There is nothing. It doesn't make sense. Do you know what happened?"

Unfortunately I was unable to offer much of an explanation. "Perhaps there's a reason. Sometimes I think Spirit wants us to rely on our senses, our feelings. Your tape might cause you to analyze too much. Go with what your heart tells you." I also felt her message from Spirit was for her ears only and wasn't to be shared with anyone else.

Several others tried to tape their sessions with me, but there were always problems. Some of the tapes came out completely blank, while the speech on others would be garbled and unintelligible. As far as I know, until John and I began working on this book, no one ever taped a session successfully. It was for that reason I always recommended that people use a pen and pad to record the most significant information. However, even that didn't always work.

One lady sat poised with her note pad as the session started. "I don't want to miss a thing," she said.

When the reading ended, I opened my eyes and was surprised to see the pad still sitting on her lap, free of any notes. "What happened," I asked.

"I don't know. I was ready to write, but I guess I forgot. I never thought about writing after you began." She shook her head and stood to leave.

"But I'll never forget what you said. I guess I didn't need to write it down."

I had no idea what had occurred or what I'd said. In those early readings, I rarely remembered what had happened. I had asked my guides that I not be a part of the experiences, feeling that the messages might be too personal or embarrassing to be known by strangers.

After being asked for clarification by many of my clients, however, I changed my mind and chose to experience the events in full consciousness. It took only a few times for me to get comfortable with the change, and, because of my being mentally present, I could offer my interpretation of what had been said. Of course I always kept everything in strict confidence.

In one of my readings I worked with a woman who had three guides, two of which were constantly chattering. Although she was unaware of the guides presence, I was certain their influence was causing her to have problems in focusing. She asked several questions, but the only answer I received was: "Tell her to look in the crystal ball."

That seemed like a ridiculous answer, and I wasn't sure about telling her what the guides had said. I felt sure I was somehow getting it wrong. At that time I had not yet learned to fully trust the messages I received, unaware that my interpretations mean little. It was easy for me to disregard what they were saying because I was focused on how I thought things should be.

I was afraid that if I repeated such a nonsensical message, the woman would think I was crazy. I argued with myself about what to tell her—later I would discover how to ignore what my brain said and to go with the answers from Spirit. The lady's message kept coming. "Tell her to look in the crystal ball."

Without placing too much emphasis on the exact words, I told her what I had received and added a comment that the guides seemed to be playful that day. I also said that I felt she needed to find a way to direct the focus of her life.

When the session ended we both walked to the front of the center. The lady paused and reached into her bag. "I want to show you something," she said. She pulled out a crystal ball.

"I purchased this recently, though at the time, I didn't know why, and I haven't shown it to anyone. I felt foolish for having bought it, but something told me to bring it with me today. I thought you might help me make sense of it. I almost fell out of my chair when you told me to look into the crystal ball."

"Obviously Spirit knew what you needed," I replied. "Use it as a tool to help you focus. I have a feeling you'll soon know its purpose."

I learned a powerful lesson that day about analyzing the messages from Spirit. And the lesson is: Don't do it. The guides will not mislead you. If you analyze your experiences, you'll often have second thoughts. Your brain is afraid of those ideas it doesn't understand, and the workings of Spirit, which are infinite, cannot be understood or explained by a finite mind. Listen with your heart, for that is the organ through which Spirit speaks.

As word spread of my readings, the number of people wanting to see me continued to increase, and not all of the requests related to humans. I once received a call from a distraught lady whose new kitten was missing. "A friend told me to call you. She said you have special powers. Can you . . . I mean, uh . . . do you see things?"

The lady explained that her kitten, "Rainbow," had been a gift from her daughter and had disappeared only three days after the daughter's death in a auto accident. "I'll never forgive myself if something happens to him. I don't know what I'll do if he's dead."

I agreed to see what I could do, although I wasn't at all certain I could help. "I'll call you in an hour," I said.

Seated in the chair I use for meditation, I asked my guides to take me to the kitten. As soon as I closed my eyes, a vision appeared of a tall building, and I heard a loud roar. I couldn't imagine what the vision represented. There were no tall buildings where the lady lived. Her house was in the country. I asked for clarification and heard a voice, "See through the animal's eyes."

Once again I tried to focus. How would I see through the eyes of the kitten? I didn't know where it was. The roaring sound and the vision of the tall building again came into my mind. See through its eyes," the voice repeated.

Suddenly it made sense. If I were a small kitten—not a human ten times its size—things would look and sound dramatically different. I imagined myself looking up from six inches above the floor. Everything would appear huge. I knew where the kitten was hiding. Only ten minutes had passed.

I excitedly called the lady. "Look behind the refrigerator. It looks like a big building."

"What?" she asked.

"The refrigerator," I repeated. "Look behind it."

"I've already checked the kitchen. I even put out some food. I'm sure he managed to get outside."

"Please look again," I insisted. "I'll wait."

A few seconds after she put down the phone, I heard her cry out. "Oh lord. It's a miracle."

She returned to the phone. "How did you know? I thought for sure I'd lost him for good. "How did you know?"

"Rainbow was just frightened. He was too terrified to move."

I listened as the lady tried to console the kitten and thank me at the same time. "Take care of him," I said. "I'm glad I could help."

I hung up and thought about what had happened. I was as puzzled as the lady was. How had I been able to connect with the energy of a kitten twenty miles across the county? I wasn't sure, but I had a warm feeling for having helped. I thanked Spirit for allowing me to share my abilities with others.

While most of my work is with people, there have been other times when animals were brought to me for help. Once I even used my healing knowledge to work with my own dog, Hans. Late one afternoon he limped to me and lay at my feet, whimpering. It was obvious from his behavior that he was in pain. After loading him in my car I drove to the veterinarian.

The doctor examined him thoroughly and told me that Hans needed surgery. "It will be expensive," he said. "Could cost a thousand dollars or more. And there's no guarantee he'll pull through."

Hans and I had been together for eight years, and he had been my best friend. Such a prognosis wasn't acceptable. "I don't think so," I said. I lifted him from the table. "There must be a better way."

"I'm sorry," the doctor said. "He'll be crippled the rest of his life. And he'll be in a lot of pain. You can take him home now, but you'll be back. There is no other way."

I put Hans back into the car and sat at the wheel sobbing. I couldn't put him through it, and yet, I didn't want to lose him.

As we drove home Maya spoke to me. "Use what you have learned. I will guide you."

Once home I helped Hans onto the sofa. He whimpered in pain as I lay him across my lap. I began stroking him and felt my hands being guided along his back and hip. Tears dripped onto his coat. Occasionally he would look up at me as if telling me he knew I was trying to help.

I continued for more than hour, then slid out from under him and went outside. Though he didn't acknowledge my leaving, he let out a long sigh as I placed his head on the sofa.

I walked through the neighborhood, wondering if I had been wrong in bringing him home. What if the vet was right? Wouldn't he have a better chance if I didn't wait? I paused at a neighbor's flower garden.

The flowers were so delicate, so beautiful. I thought about our place in the universe. Every living thing is surely God's creation, and if so, wouldn't God be willing to use His power to help if we only asked in faith.

"Let go of the doubt," I heard. "Let go of fear."

I ran home and jerked open the door. Hans greeted me by jumping against my chest. His wagging tail and enthusiastic welcome told me he was okay. I held him as we danced around the room. "Thank you," I whispered.

Hans lived with me for three more years with no further problems. Later, when I decided to move away, I thought it best to return him to the lady who had given him to me. I knew he would be well cared for, and though I never heard from him again, I was confident that the angels continued to watch over him.

I've only been asked to work with animals a few times, though I never encourage it, for one of the allergies I've suffered from is pet dander. Even today cats sometimes cause me to have an allergic reaction. The times I've worked with them, however, my allergies have never bothered me. The healing energy seems to overcome any problem I might have with animals; when working with them, I don't experience a reaction.

I know I'm protected. My willingness to allow myself to be used as an instrument for healing transcends any negative energy. My work is the reason I was returned to this life, and I'm ready to offer my help to all those who are ready for healing.

Being available for readings, though, is a different situation. While people seemed to benefit, I often wondered if what I was doing really helped in their growth. After much thought and prayer, I decided to limit the number I would do.

Eventually, I stopped doing them altogether. Many of those who came to me seemed to be searching for easy solutions to their problems. They wanted me to call upon God or the spirits to change their lives without their having to do the work themselves.

I don't like telling people no, for I can't see what is best for each person. If they ask for help, I want to give it if I can. One day, however, Maya reminded me of the two parts to my mission. "Remember to teach," she said. "You must not try to do the work for others. Your task is to show them what they should do and then to allow them the freedom to choose. It is time to begin the next part of your journey."

CHAPTER 9

My Mission

With my work at the metaphysical center over I asked my guides to show me what I was to do next. I was certain there was something more meaningful for me, but I didn't know how to find it. The changes I had made seemed incomplete, and I struggled with how I would continue molding the new me. The way I viewed the world—the way I viewed everything—was in turmoil, and though I didn't understand all that was happening, I felt it crucial that I live in a manner compatible with my ever-changing awareness.

The work I'd done with others, as well as my reading and studying, had dramatically altered my awareness. Life had made a complete reversal, though its ultimate direction seemed undetermined. I knew things would never be the same as before and I didn't want them to be.

I was filled with wonder for the world in which I existed and eager to move forward, wherever that might be. I also wanted to make better use of the healing techniques I had learned. I prayed for guidance.

One of the first things I realized was that my life was too complicated and I had accumulated far too much stuff. As a corporate manager my goal had been to have a new outfit for each day of the year, and though my wardrobe had never grown to such ridiculous proportions, my closet, as well as the rest of my house, overflowed with much that was unnecessary.

I donated and gave away many of the things I had spent years gathering, and I did it gladly, relishing the feelings that accompanied my new-found generosity. Not only was I comforted in the knowledge that others would benefit from the things I was discarding, I was also invigorated by an incredible feeling of buoyancy. I felt as if a great burden had been lifted. The experience seemed to be a cleansing, unmasking my true self. But I soon realized that disposing of things was not enough. A complete cleansing would mean getting rid of our house. It was much too large for our needs and as I was no longer employed, it was a drain on our resources. After discussing the alternatives we decided to sell and move into an apartment. Our expenses would be reduced and we would have more time to relax and enjoy living. Mike had never been enthusiastic about yard work and was eager to have more time to further his computer skills.

Within a few months we located an apartment that seemed just right for the two of us, and we moved shortly thereafter. For the first few months the apartment was great. Our sparse furnishings made the place easy to maintain, and we relished the extra time our new, more compact home afforded.

Soon, however, it became obvious that I not only needed to rid myself of the trappings of my old life, I needed to separate myself from the congestion and turmoil that was an inherent part of living in the city. I longed for the fresh air and quiet of the country. Once again I approached my husband with my dilemma. And once more he surprised me with his support and eagerness to assist in my evolution.

I wanted to be close to nature. In its quiet I hoped to discover where Spirit was leading me. Another layer of the illusion was being peeled away as a new dimension to my life was being added.

As soon as Mike and I began discussing our options, it was evident that a home in the country was still a home, with perhaps even more responsibilities than our previous one. We struggled with our dilemma for weeks until one day I developed what I considered the best solution. When he came home that afternoon I cautiously approached him with my idea. We would buy a motor home, a small one that would be easy to maintain, one we could easily move whenever we wished. It seemed the perfect way to resolve our problem.

He agreed, and his support was unconditional. I adore the wonderful way he indulges me and my unorthodox ideas. He is one of the many gifts Spirit has bestowed upon me. I am truly blessed.

Within days we were searching the dealers and ads looking for a small motor home in good condition, and we soon found one that seemed a perfect fit. We bought it on the spot. Moving in, however, proved to be more difficult than I had expected. Though I had given away most of the stuff I felt unnecessary, I was far from being ready for motor home life. Almost everything had to go. We were limited to only a few outfits each, and the things we could keep had to be pint-sized, from the TV to the microwave. Our second downsizing seemed to be a continuation of my spiritual growth, and Mike, in his calm, good-natured way, eagerly went along without objection.

Finding the camper, though, was only half the solution; we also had to locate a place to park it. A few months earlier a friend had taken me on a visit to a campground near Dahlonega, a picturesque community in the north Georgia mountains. "I don't know why, but I want you to see this place," she had said.

I wasn't particularly impressed. The setting was pretty and offered spectacular views of the surrounding mountains, but it was just a campground, something I didn't need at that time. I had no idea I might one day be searching for just such a place.

I called my friend and had her refresh my memory on the park's location. Two days later Mike and I drove up and picked out a site. "It's perfect," he said. It's not too far from my work, yet secluded enough so that you can clear your mind." We rented a space and were soon enjoying both the benefits and struggles of our new lifestyle.

Once we settled into our new neighborhood, I began making friends with those who, like us, were more permanent residents. I told them little about my past, unsure how they might accept it.

Mother's warnings were still instilled in my memory, and I didn't want to be stoned by my neighbors.

However, I did hope to be given an opportunity to use the healing methods I had learned, for I had a sincere desire to help those who were in need. I just wasn't comfortable in announcing to my new friends that they could come to me for healing and had no idea how to present the subject. However, in the years that have followed I've discovered that Spirit always has a way to assist us when we listen and respond. Soon thereafter the opportunity to help others appeared.

One evening as we visited with our neighbors, Bob and Mary, a powerful thunderstorm began to develop. Bob stepped to the window, watching the approaching storm. As he stood there a terrific bolt of lightening struck a large pine tree less than twenty feet from his trailer. The intense flash and powerful clap of thunder shook the room and Bob staggered back, falling across a chair. "I can't see," he said as we helped him onto the sofa. "My eyes are on fire."

Bob had served in Vietnam and had never fully recovered from a shrapnel injury that affected his nervous system. The intense brightness of the lightening strike appeared to have overloaded optic nerves already weakened by illness. Not only was he unable to see, he appeared to be in severe pain.

I hesitated only a moment and then stepped closer to him. I placed my hand under his chin and lifted his face towards mine. As I looked down I felt Maya's presence. I knew I had to do something, and at that moment I didn't care what the consequences might be. I just wanted to help.

"Do you want to be healed?" I asked. "Are you ready to be healed, regardless of how that healing comes?"

The room was silent. Even the storm seemed to pause. I looked towards Bob's wife who was seated next to him. Though she had a puzzled look, she smiled. "Can you do something?" she asked.

An incredible sense of confidence filled me as I responded. "I can't, but the angels can, the angels who are here with us now."

I gently rubbed my fingers across Bob's forehead. Beads of perspiration had formed and his brow wrinkled with obvious pain. "Do you truly want to be healed?" I asked again. "Open your eyes."

He nodded and mumbled, "Yes, whatever you can do. Please do it." There was uncertainty in his voice.

I worked with him for more than thirty minutes, each movement guided by my angel friends. While my hands massaged his temples, I mentally scanned his energy field, pausing occasionally to flick my fingers towards the floor, removing some unknown matter that seemed to accumulate on them. As I worked, I felt as if I had returned to one of my special dreams. The visions and sensations I experienced made it seem that I was in two locations at once, both in my body and, at the same time, hovering somewhere above. For me, the experience was powerful beyond comprehension. Never before had I felt my angel guides in such a manner.

When I sensed the treatment was finished, I felt Maya slip away. As soon as she was gone, my body jerked and I returned to normal consciousness.

Mike, who had been sitting next to Mary during the healing, was the first to speak. "Are you okay honey? Your face is all red."

"I'm great," I said, "a little dazed, but really energized." I eased onto the sofa to try to grasp what had happened.

I turned to Bob and Mary. They were holding hands. "That was more powerful than the lightening," Bob said. "It felt like electricity was coming out of your hands. How did you do that?"

"Can you see?" his wife asked. "How are your eyes?"

"They still burn a little, and everything's all blurry. But I can see. Praise God."

Bob's vision continued to improve during the coming days, although he still reported experiencing some pain. However, his sight had returned to normal within a few weeks. Although he began to refer to me as the "healer lady," he never questioned what I had done and never discussed the strange events of that evening.

Another of my neighbors, Sue, had been confined to a wheelchair following back surgery. Soon after Bob's healing she approached me. "Do you think you can help me," she asked, "like you did Bob? I've been this way for more than ten years, and it just gets worse. The doctors describe it as a degeneration of the bone. All I know is it hurts a lot."

At first I wasn't sure what to say, but the words seemed to come out without thought. "Yes, we'll see what we can do. We can do it together. I'll show you how to call on the angels, and your body will remember how to heal itself."

I leaned down and placed my hands on her legs. They were incredibly cold and lifeless. I said a prayer asking the angels to guide us and to remove any doubts that she could be healed. Immediately, I felt the presence of Maya, although I didn't mention it to Sue.

I worked with her for about an hour, first moving my hands about her legs, from her hips to her feet. Later, I knelt behind her and slipped my hands onto the base of her spine. When I heard Maya say, "It is done," I felt her energy leave. I stood and told Sue we were finished. "But we'll do this every day for the next week," I said.

She leaned forward as if she wanted to get up. "Don't try it now. Give it time," I said. "You'll begin to feel a difference."

"Oh, I feel a difference now. My legs feel better than they have in years."

We met as planned for the next week, then changed the healing sessions to only twice a week. Within a month we were doing them weekly.

Two months after we had begun, Sue phoned me. "Come over here," she said. "I want to show you something." She giggled as she spoke.

A few minutes later I knocked on her door. She pulled open the door and rolled back her wheelchair as she had always done.

"What's the big news," I asked. Sue looked up with a broad smile.

"Watch this." As she spoke, she pushed up from her chair and took three steps toward me. She held out her arms. "Look at me. I'm walking."

She grabbed me, and we stood there sobbing, hugging each other, and laughing.

"It's a miracle," she said.

"Yes it is," I responded. "But it's one you can do now that you know you have the power. You don't need me anymore. Ask the angels to guide you. They're here with us now. Call on them and you'll find new strength."

It wasn't long afterwards that Sue moved away, but I knew she would be okay. She had rediscovered her connection with the angels, and I had begun to realize my mission to teach and heal.

CHAPTER 10

A Larger Audience

A few weeks after the experience with Sue, my work took a new turn when I received a call from a woman who said she was a TV producer. "We're doing a one-hour special about angels and healers and would like to feature you in a segment. Can I come up and explain what we want to do?"

"I don't think so," I said.

"It might be good for you. You'll get national exposure."

"That's the last thing I want. How did you get in touch with me?"

"I'm not sure. One of the producers gave me a list of names and yours was on it. Would you at least consider being on the show?"

"I don't want to be on TV," I said. "I enjoy my privacy. That's why I moved to the mountains."

The lady on the phone was persistent. "Think about it and I'll call you back in a couple of days. I don't want to push, but I'll need to know soon. I have a schedule, you know."

I hung up the phone. Television. I didn't even like to watch it. I sure didn't want to be on it.

That evening I prayed for guidance. If the producer had found me, perhaps she had been guided. I asked the angels for help.

The answer I received was clear. "If one person is helped, would it not be worth it?"

Yes, I thought, of course it would.

Three days later I received another call from Susan, the producer. I agreed to do the show, but said she would have to come to me. I didn't want to go back to the city for any reason.

"Is there someone there you can perform a healing on?" she asked.

"No. If we're going to do this, I don't want there to be any doubts about whether or not it's genuine. The person should be a stranger. You'll have to find them."

Two weeks had passed when several cars, followed by a large truck, pulled into the campground. Susan stepped out and introduced herself.

"We found a lady in Marietta, suffering from cancer, and she has agreed to allow us to film you working with her. Her condition is pretty serious, and the doctors have given her little hope. She's willing to try anything to be healed. Do you think it's okay? Maybe you can help her."

Yes, I was eager to help, but I wasn't looking for publicity. I'd never intended to use my healing gifts to become famous or as a way to make money.

I was introduced to Betty, the lady with cancer, and to the members of the film crew. As I guided them to a secluded area in the woods behind the park, I tried to convey my feelings about what we were doing. "What I do comes from God," I said. "It must be honored and treated with respect. Whether or not you understand or believe in what I'm doing, I hope you will do as I ask."

I stopped and pointed into a small clearing. "We'll work here." One of the crew had carried my table and helped me set it up.

An hour later they were ready, cables stretched back to their generator, bright lights everywhere, and cameras set up and ready to roll. "When I am working," I said, "I must ask that you not enter into the circle. Point your cameras anywhere you wish, but do not come beyond this point." I drew an imaginary line around the table.

The lead cameraman rolled his eyes. Earlier I had felt negative energy from him and had sensed his lack of belief. I wasn't concerned and ignored him.

"You can get on the table now," I said to Betty. "We will begin."

I hadn't noticed how frail she was when they had first arrived, but walking the short distance into the woods she had required assistance. One of the crew helped her onto the table. She winced with each movement, and when she spoke, her voice was hardly audible.

"I have an angel who has come to help me," she whispered. "He appeared to me in the hospital." She smiled and closed her eyes.

Soon after I began working with her, I realized what she meant. There standing at the end of the table, with wings outstretched towards heaven, was one of the most beautiful creatures I've ever seen. Her angel had indeed come to help.

The healing was also assisted by a mountain lion who came and lay across Betty's chest. He remained there, motionless, during the entire healing process. Maya came and was joined by Walks with Moon, and the healing was both powerful and energizing.

When it was finished I put my hands behind Betty's head to help her up. "I don't need help," she said as she raised up and eased off the table. "I feel wonderful. Whatever you did made a difference, and when you pressed on my chest I was filled with energy. I didn't tell her that my hands were never on her chest, assuming she had felt the power of the mountain lion I had seen.

Betty returned two more times. The pain had almost gone, she said, and she appeared much stronger. "I'm not afraid to die, but there are two things I have to do before I leave. I need the strength to finish them; then I can go."

On her third visit, she brought her minister. She was excited about her progress, and said her doctor couldn't believe how she had improved. "They interviewed him for the TV show and he told them he couldn't explain why so much of the cancer had disappeared."

Her minister was more skeptical. As soon as we met, I felt he had come to discredit my work. His intentions were good—he wanted to protect Betty—but he couldn't acknowledge that God would work in such an unusual way. During the healing session he watched carefully, perhaps looking for some sort of trickery. When I was finished, he quizzed me about my methods.

"How do you know what to do? And where does your healing power come from?"

"I'm guided by the spirits, by power that ultimately comes from God," I said. "Everything I do comes from God."

"I hope you're not offended if I speak frankly. You're not at all what I expected. Although Betty told me you didn't ask for money, I was sure you had ulterior motives. Now, I'm not so sure."

I could tell he was struggling—as so many of us do—to understand how God could work in ways far beyond what we have been taught is possible. "Don't worry," I said. "You're not the first skeptic I've encountered."

After talking for another hour he told me he had to go. "Thanks for taking time to explain what you do. I still don't know what I think, but I do believe God is somehow working through you. I'd like to bring my wife up here if you don't mind. Maybe you can help with her back problem. The doctors sure haven't."

I saw Betty only one more time. A few months after our first meeting I received a call that she was in the hospital and had asked if I would come by the next day. I didn't know how I would be able to go, for three people had made appointments to see me that day. I told the caller to tell her I was sorry, and that I would try to come in a day or two.

But Spirit knew when I needed to be there. All three of my appointments called and cancelled that afternoon, and the following day I drove to the hospital as requested.

Betty's doctor was with her when I walked into the room. "We can try another treatment," he said. "We still have some powerful drugs in our arsenal."

"There's no time," she responded. "I'll be gone in forty-eight hours."

Her doctor tried to comfort her, but she waived him off. "You'll see. I can leave now. My work is done."

I spent a few minutes with her, and she thanked me for what I had done. "I couldn't have made it without you," she said. "You gave me the strength to finish my work."

I was grateful for having been given the opportunity to serve, and tried to explain how I felt honored that she had allowed me to help her. I left knowing I would never see her again, and sent a prayer that she would be guided in her transition to a new life.

Betty died the following day. Having lived far longer than the doctors had predicted, she had received the strength to complete the work she felt compelled to do.

One of the most wonderful of all those who have come to me for healing was Kyle, a young cancer patient whose parents called me on Monday after the TV show had aired. Though they lived hundreds of miles away, they wanted to know if they could bring Kyle to see me the following weekend. I sensed desperation in the mother's voice.

After agreeing to see their son I asked the angels what I was to do. Their answer showed me that my purpose for working with Kyle would be to prepare his parents for what was to come. The boy was ready and would be leaving soon. Until then the angels would help him to be more comfortable.

When the three arrived I took them to the small building that had been converted for my work. Once inside I had Kyle climb onto the table. His bald head displayed a scar from one side to the other, an unsuccessful attempt, his dad later told me, to remove the tumor that had entrenched itself in his brain.

Kyle looked up apprehensively. "You're not going to stick me, are you?" His beautiful brown eyes conveyed the pain I knew he had suffered.

"No, I'm not going to hurt you at all. I hope I can help to stop the hurting."

"Me too," he said. And then he said the most unusual thing, something I would later realize to be true. "You know I'm already an angel. I really am."

I worked with Kyle, and he and his parents returned several more times. He was right; he was an angel, one sent with a special task that was nearing completion. I couldn't tell his parents, but I'm sure they felt it too. They just weren't ready to give him up.

A little more than a year later I was sitting outside the RV bathing myself in the fresh air and sunshine, when a cool breeze blew across my face. I felt a gentle kiss on my cheek. "I just wanted to say goodbye," I heard Kyle's soft voice. An hour later his dad called. "Kyle is gone."

It's hard for us to accept it when such angels come to us only to suffer and eventually die. It's difficult because we can't understand. We're trapped in a body bound to earth and we can't see into infinity. We have to trust and be glad for the experiences of love and joy that life on earth brings.

I'm saddened when my efforts don't result in healing, for there are still times when I too question why life is as it is. I can't take away the pain when a loved one dies, and I can't offer a suitable explanation. My task is to help others discover their true self, the Divine within. Once that is realized, the temporary pains of this life are seen for what they are—at the most, nothing.

CHAPTER 11

Following the Still Small Voice

One morning I awoke and went to the small box where Mike and I kept our emergency money. Whenever either of us was short of cash and needed something, we would just take the amount we needed. Each month after paying our bills we would put whatever money remained into the box.

That morning, however, I didn't need anything. I still had a few dollars in my purse. Yet something compelled me to pull the box from its shelf. As I slid it onto the table a voice said, "Count it."

The voice was so clear that I spoke aloud, "Why?"

"Count it," the voice repeated.

How strange, I thought. I'd never counted it and didn't care how much money there was. I couldn't recall either of us ever checking to see how much we had.

When I finished counting, I returned the box back to its shelf, wondering why it had seemed so important to know how much we had. When Mike came home that evening I understood. "What do you think about going on an adventure?" he asked. "I turned in my resignation today. I don't know where I'd like to go, but I think we should get away for a while. Let's see how much money we've saved." He reached for the box.

"I can tell you," I said. "I didn't know why at the time, but I counted it this morning."

We talked about places we might go, but didn't come to a decision. "Let's just leave," I said. "We can figure it out as we drive."

Living in a motor home sometimes has its advantages, and two weeks later, we disconnected and pulled away. Driving west we toured several states before stopping in Cottonwood, a small town in northern Arizona. We were familiar with the area, having stayed nearby a couple of years before while on vacation. I had even made a solo return trip a year later—a trip I had been guided to take—and had spent a few nights in Cottonwood.

During both my previous trips I'd had some unusual experiences, prophetic visions of things I'd see and places I'd later visit. The energy of the place is so powerful that it's become a Mecca for new-age seekers. On the trip I had taken alone the year before, I had been awakened at 3:00 A.M. and instructed to walk behind my hotel. Never having been much of a risk taker, I was reluctant to follow their advice. I was unfamiliar with thc area, didn't know if it was safe, and was concerned about snakes and other critters that might be roaming about. I tried to negotiate with the guides, offered to go after sunrise or to look out my bathroom window which faced the rear of the hotel.

The guides, of course, ignored my protests and continued to persuade. When I finally gave in, I slipped on my robe and walked behind the hotel. The night air was cool, and the sky was ablaze with millions of stars. Following directions that seemed spoken inside my head, I walked a short distance into the desert. At some point I stopped and looked up. The view was incredible. Everything was so clear. As I gazed skyward, the stars disappeared and a wonderful city took their place. It didn't seem like one of my visions; it was so real. It floated above me, yet I saw the city both as a whole and at the same time into its streets and houses. There were children playing ball, moving it with their minds and plants growing on crystals that were suspended in mid air.

It was a view of Shambhala, or Shangri-La, that mystical city we all long to discover. The difference was, I had not traveled through the snows and mountains to find it, my guides had brought it to me. I looked on in wonder and amazement and realized that the peace and harmony of that place is here for us to create in each of our lives. We don't have to travel to distant lands; it isn't necessary to go anywhere. Shangri-La is here if we will acknowledge it.

An hour later I returned to my room. I thanked the angels for showing me where true peace was to be found. I had a dreamless and restful sleep for the remainder of the night.

The following morning I dressed and again walked to the rear of the hotel. I suppose I somehow hoped something of my vision remained. When I looked to the area where I had walked, I was amazed to see that it was completely impassible. A deep gorge cut through the desert, its walls much too steep for me to have climbed. Nothing appeared as it had the night before. Yet, I was sure I had gone out, my shoes were scuffed and filled with sand. I was left to ponder what had happened, with confirmation that much of the world we experience cannot be understood.

Much of that part of northern Arizona is surrounded in mystery. The Native Americans held it sacred and regularly made pilgrimages there, and the ancient ones did cave paintings that depicted ancestral beings floating in the air. For me it is a powerful place that can help us to connect with our inner strength and wisdom. I had hoped that my third trip, especially because I was making an extended stay, would help me discover more of my mission.

Mike seemed attracted to the area too, perhaps for different reasons, and we decided to make it our new home. We had no idea how long we would stay, but realized it could be long enough for us to need extra money. Mike suggested he try to find a job, and two days later he drove into Cottonwood and found one, working in a local electronics shop.

We had been there a couple of months when I received a call from a TV station in Los Angeles. "We have a weekly show here, called *The Other Side*, and would like to have you appear on it. It's about miracles, the supernatural, and psychic phenomena. Would you consider coming here and taping a segment?"

Once again I was curious how they had located me, especially so far from home, but I didn't even bother to ask. If they had called, I assumed I should do it. I agreed and was flown to California where I did participate in the show, but it was nothing like the one I had taped in Georgia. The energy of the studio, the lights, the audience, the confusion—none of it felt good.

I also made most of the other participants angry when the moderator asked me how much I charged for a healing. "Nothing," I responded. "I don't feel I should charge for something I received as a gift from God."

Riding the bus back to our hotel, I was verbally assaulted for my views on not charging fees for my work. "How dare you make us look so greedy," one said. "This is the way I make a living."

I apologized for having offended anyone, and explained that my husband's work provided for us. "I'm grateful for both his emotional and financial support and that I don't have to depend on my healing work for income. Any power that I have to heal has come to me as a gift, and I'm not comfortable in asking others to pay for my help. If someone does give me money, I share it with those I know need it more. Just as you have chosen your path, I have chosen mine, and no one else can know if our choice is correct."

When the bus pulled into the hotel, my companions were still mumbling about how I had embarrassed them. I was thankful the ride was over and promised myself not to do a TV show again.

The next day I returned to Arizona, glad to be away from the city and back in the peaceful quiet of our desert home. The energy of the place seemed to help me focus, helped me to peel away the layers of illusion that I'd accumulated. At night I would look at the stars and strengthen my connection with a world I'd ignored for decades. Mike loved the place too, and for that reason he was surprised when he came home one day and found me crying. "We've got to go back to Georgia," I said.

"What is it? Are you homesick?"

"No. This is our home; we brought it with us. Anywhere we're together is fine with me. But something is pulling me back. I don't know why, but we have to leave now."

Mike is so wonderful and understanding. He called his boss and explained that we were leaving, and we started home the next morning.

Leaving on short notice we decided not to tell friends or family that we were coming—our return would be a surprise; but as we neared Alabama, I asked him to detour to his mom's house. "I don't know why, but we need to stop."

When we pulled into the drive, her car was gone. "We'll have to wait," I said. I knew she would return soon.

"I have a key," Mike said. "We can wait inside."

We were hardly through the door when the phone rang. It was my friend Beverly. She was shocked when I answered the phone. "I tried to reach you in Arizona," she said. "I even talked with the park manager, but he said he didn't know where you were going. Your dad is in the hospital. He had a heart attack yesterday, and he's not doing well. I was calling Mike's mom to see if she knew where you were. God, I'm so glad I could reach you."

I explained that we had left three days earlier and had planned our return to be a surprise. "I knew we needed to come home, but I wasn't sure why."

We drove to the hospital the next day, and I hurried to dad's room. He looked so helpless. Always trying to be strong, he had never complained, though in later years I knew he tried to hide the pain that made it difficult for him to walk. I couldn't remember when he had ever admitted being sick. I suppose his Cherokee heritage made him feel he could not show weakness.

I asked Maya to help me bring healing to him. Though the hospital staff gave me some curious looks, I didn't care. I was being guided by the angels.

Three days later he was released. The doctors couldn't explain his dramatic recovery, but I knew. I was thankful the angels had told me to come home. I was growing accustomed to hearing their sometimes subtle urgings and could see the results.

Not all of my experiences have been so positive. Some of my visions have come from what appears to be a bleak and ominous future. Smoke billows from crumbling cities and the ground trembles with violent earthquakes. In those scenes the sun is obscured by a sky blackened with smoke and ash.

While the feeling I have from those visions is depressing, I sense that the scene is but one possible future, that we still have the opportunity to change our course. If we continue to be guided by greed and selfishness, such a future may be inevitable. However, if we can begin learning how to honor our earth mother and each other, the destruction can be avoided. I hope we choose the latter path.

Several years ago I had an experience that may be connected to my visions of the future. I was reading a book and came upon an equation I interpreted as a means of calculating when I would die. Although I'm not mathematically inclined, never liked math or algebra in school, I was fascinated by the way the formula worked and was eager to share it with Mike when he came home.

As soon as dinner was finished, I excitedly grabbed the book and told him about my discovery. I thumbed through the pages to the section where I had been reading. The formula wasn't there! I looked back through the previous chapters. Nothing! The next day I re-read the entire book, but was unable to find a reference to anything resembling what I had been shown.

At that time I concluded that Spirit had used the book as a way to help me focus, and I had received the information to show me how much time there was for me to complete my work. Lately, however, I've begun to wonder if my interpretation as the time of my death is correct. Perhaps it's only an indication of a dramatic shift I'll experience, maybe a warning that the time for action has come.

Strangely, the date the formula showed me coincides with the predictions of Mayan and other ancient prophecies. Perhaps it represents my connection with the dramatic changes such prophecies foretell. If humankind is to survive, I must do my part.

I keep it in mind as I continue. However, I'm not morbid about the possibility of death. If that is what it represents, I give thanks that Spirit has provided me with sufficient time and the means to accomplish my goals.

CHAPTER 12

Sharing the Lessons

The angels had told me I would teach and heal, and I still remember waking in the emergency room questioning: "Teach what?" I had no training and no experience in teaching anything. My career had been in management, but I was never asked to do training. How would I teach things I was still learning?

My friend, Beverly, provided an answer. "You need to do workshops. You've learned so much that others would like to know. I'll help if you'll let me."

"I don't know," I said. "I received this gift without charge. How can I use it to make money? And I don't like speaking in public."

The idea of doing workshops was unlike anything I had ever imagined. Would people really be interested in learning about my experiences? I was especially uncomfortable with making people pay for knowledge that I felt should be given for free.

"Charge as little as you like, but if you want to reach a greater number of people, you'll have to do something. And if you do it, you'll have to rent space. There will be costs involved, but that doesn't mean it has to be expensive. As far as the speaking goes, all you have to do is talk to the people. Tell them like you told me. Teach them what you learned from the angels."

I finally agreed to let her schedule a workshop, but I never thought she would be able to do it. Where would she find enough people to make it work? However, I underestimated Beverly's passion and tenacity. After all, the angels had been teaching her too.

Of course we did have the workshop, and I was pleased with the results. I was far less nervous than I had imagined. It was just like talking to a group of my best friends—and after the workshop many of us were.

Afterwards, I received several nice comments from the participants. "Thank you," one said. "I've always wanted to know about healing. My father has been sick for years, and I feel so helpless. You've shown me how I can help him. God bless you."

It wasn't long after the first one that I did another, then another. Word spread about the workshops, and I began to receive calls about doing them in other locations. I had found a way to share what I had learned with a larger audience who could in turn pass what they had learned to others.

Because we kept our costs to a minimum, we were able to charge only a modest fee, and those who were unable to pay were allowed to attend for free. I only asked that they put what they learned into practice and teach it to friends and family.

A few months later Beverly approached me with another suggestion. "There are so many times I wish you could just be with me. Your calming energy always helps to keep things in perspective. What if you made a tape of some of the lessons? That way you could be available whenever anyone needed you."

Though I had no idea how to begin, I asked for guidance, and the angels told me they would help. Beverly found a recording studio and offered to pay for the session. The day of recording I was put in a soundproof booth, "Watch the glass," the producer said. "We'll signal you when it's time to wrap it up."

"I won't see you," I said. "I'll be in prayer."

"What if I come and tap on the glass?"

"No, not until I tell you it's okay," I responded. Being interrupted didn't seem appropriate. "I'll let you know when I'm done." I knew the angels would make sure that everything went okay.

"Begin when I signal you," he said. "But somehow you'll have to know when to stop."

I told him not to be concerned. I wasn't sure how much more I should say. He shrugged his shoulders and walked to his equipment.

I had no plan or written script, for the lessons don't come from me. I'm just the messenger. I closed my eyes and asked the angels to come in. Maya immediately appeared and began teaching her breath techniques. Later, Walks With Moon came and sang some healing songs. When they had finished, I opened my eyes.

"Perfect," the technician yelled. "I don't know how you knew when to stop, but it's just perfect." He may not have known, but I did. I had trusted the angels, and as always, they knew exactly what to do.

How did I learn to attune myself to their sometimes subtle messages and urgings? How did I learn to recognize and trust their voices? It didn't happen overnight. I first had to learn how to quiet the self-talk, and getting quiet took a lot of practice.

In the years since my death experience, I've learned that the angels want me to share as much of what I learned as possible. For me that is the significance of my life on earth. We're all potential teachers. Once we learn how to communicate with the angels, and to listen to the true self, we have an obligation to teach others. Healing, while important, is only a part of the experience. When we become aware of our divine nature, we will naturally want to help others do the same.

In the remaining chapters, I will explain some of the healing techniques I learned, but I will also share what the angels taught me about discovering the true self and how we fit into our wondrous universe. As grand as that sounds, it's really a simple task. If my words can only cause the reader to stop seeing him/herself as separate, catching a brief glimpse of their divine nature, then I have succeeded. Once acknowledged, the experience cannot be denied.

The first step is to discover the identity of our true self. I will share some of the ways the angels taught me to communicate with my subconscious, my inner pilot who knows both my path and destination.

The way to begin is through a daily practice of meditation. What is meditation and why do we need to do it? Meditation puts us in touch with reality, and the reason we need to do it is that most of us are out of touch. We live in a world of symbols, a world described in words and pictures that are created in our brains.

Just as we confuse who we are with our name, our occupation, our position relative to others, we confuse the real world with the names, the words, we have assigned to it. We live in a world where the symbols of things are accepted as the things themselves. Our world is like a never-ending Disneyland where everything appears real, but is no more than plastic replicas. However, in the real world there are neither things nor events; there is only being, and the connectedness of everything in our experience.

And that is the beginning of our problems. We stress ourselves, become frustrated and angry because we have lost touch with the only things of importance. We fill our minds with thoughts, meaningless streams of words about what we have done or should do, what others have done or should do, to or for us, and all the while we plod through our lives searching for the meaning.

Our search for what is real leads us to accumulating a vast array of the symbols of reality, and yet, the more symbols we gather, the more difficult it becomes for us to be able to recognize reality when we see it.

The best way I know to experience reality is through meditation. But most of us have tried meditation—usually with disappointing results. What does it have to offer that we've not already experienced?

To begin with, it's one of the most powerful tools to discovering true peace. The disappointment we may have experienced in the past was probably caused by a lack of understanding of what meditation is—and, more importantly, is not. It is not a way to accomplish anything, and it doesn't have a purpose. It's not a solemn prayer to the God above or within, and it's not a way of achieving nirvana.

Although that statement may sound contradictory, when we begin to understand exactly what meditation is, the meaning becomes more clear. Meditation helps us to get out of our own way so that we may feel our basic connection with everything else. As we meditate, wonderful experiences may occur, but the meditation itself does not bring those things about. For instance, if we attempt to have a purpose in our meditation, we're not meditating. It's like composing or playing music. If we are listening to someone playing the piano, there is no purpose. We listen for the enjoyment of it.

Where do we begin? The first step is to quiet the continuing mind chatter, the never ending conversations that we hold with ourselves. When we talk, we cannot hear what others have to say. In the same way when we think, we cannot hear what the Universe has to teach us. Talking and thinking keep us in the world of symbols and out of touch with reality.

Meditation gives us the opportunity to learn from the Universe and to be aware of our relationship with it. Not only does it allow us to feel our Oneness, it helps us to understand the meaning of the Eternal Now, that there is no past, no future. There is only the present.

Is there a correct posture for meditation? Not really, though there are some basic elements that should be followed. You should sit erect, either on the floor or in a chair, but you should not lie down. Trying to meditate in bed or lying on a sofa will train your body to go to sleep instead of meditation.

There are also some tools that can be used to assist in your journey. The sound of a gong, a drum, the relaxing sounds of flowing water, or waves crashing on a beach are some of the tools that will help you reach a meditative state. And the smell of incense will trigger that part of the brain that brings about relaxation and releases the stress of the day. And, of course, the breath can be used to guide you into meditation. Chapter thirteen describes several breath techniques in greater detail.

It's best to begin meditation with a series of deep breaths to cleanse both the body and Spirit. Breathe deeply into the deepest part of your lungs, filling them to maximum capacity, and then slowly release the air, blowing gently through slightly parted lips. Do a minimum of ten breaths. Once you have completed the breaths, allow your lungs to pull in the air they need, finding the rhythm that is comfortable. Begin to count the out breaths and watch as your breathing gets slower and slower. Continue breathing and counting until you have reached one hundred. As you count, if you become aware that you have lost count and have begun thinking, once more begin your count at the number one. Don't be concerned if you have to do this many times. You aren't competing with anyone, especially yourself. You are training yourself to allow your mind to connect with Spirit. It will take time.

When thoughts interrupt you, hear them just as you would hear the sound of splashing water or a gong. Your thoughts are no different from all the sensory input your brain receives—the sounds of the birds, traffic outside, the ringing of the phone, footsteps nearby—all are signals transmitted to the brain. Don't try to name them, to identify them, just observe them and let them go on.

Notice that as your breathing continues it becomes slower, easier; it seems to fall in and out of its own accord. Sometimes it is helpful to chant, to create a sound that assists in the meditation. You might try to hum slightly on the out breath. Don't try to create a particular sound—one sound is no better than another—just allow your breath to generate a slight hum as it goes out of the lungs.

Let your mind be like a mountain stream. Let it flow—gently, and without conscious effort. Let whatever happens, happen. It isn't necessary to force results and you shouldn't try to obstruct what comes. Just be. Whatever you choose to do is correct. Wherever your mind goes is where it should be. Allow the barriers of ego to fall away. You are perfect.

Both the optimist and the pessimist are right. We are the creators of our worlds. Within each of us lies the power to bring into our lives whatever we wish. The seeming lack of what we desire is only one of understanding. What we lack is harmony with our Divine Self, the part that many call God and often think of as separate.

If we can only learn to change our thoughts, we will transform the world as we know it, and our lives will be expressions of peace. But changing our thoughts doesn't come about through effort. You can spend a lifetime—a thousand lifetimes—trying to alter the way you think and it may never happen. The way to lasting change is through awareness of self, and that comes in quiet reflection, in giving your true nature its rightful position of power.

CHAPTER 13

Listening to the Body

Do you believe that Spirit or God is good, is all powerful, all knowing, and is with us always? I do. Yet, while many would agree that He is aware of the smallest part of their existence, they live as if the opposite is true. Why do we feel it necessary to constantly remind Spirit of our needs, especially those that concern our physical well being? Why do we fill our prayers with pleadings to help us, or those close to us, to overcome pain, illness, or disease?

Why? We do so, I believe, because we don't see our divine nature, our connection with our Creator. We either think we're not worthy of God's awareness of our condition or assume our connection to have been broken by past sins, or worse, the sins of our ancestors.

I found a better way. Instead of spending my time reminding an all-knowing Creator of what is obviously already known, my angel guides taught me how to listen to my body to discover its needs and the source of its problems. Once I learned how to attune myself to the physical, I could see what was going on, what problems existed, and could understand what I needed to do about it. By listening instead of talking I stay in touch with my body, know what foods best maintain health, what type of exercise I need, and can immediately recognize when special attention is required.

The angels showed me how to connect with and listen to the bodies of others. With their guidance I learned how to tune into the energy, the messages that our bodies continually send out. Since we are made of energy, and since our brains and our hearts both have the ability to send and receive energy, we can learn how to receive messages from others. We can tune ourselves to their frequency, just like tuning a radio, and absorb anything the other person is willing to share. The willingness is not necessarily a conscious effort but an agreement in the world of Spirit.

Once I learned how to listen, I was able to actually see inside the bodies of others. I could see their organs, in full color, and could easily detect those that were malfunctioning or diseased. Seeing the body in that way allowed me to know what was necessary to return it to a proper healthy condition. The body, I discovered, is continually communicating exactly what it needs. Understanding how to listen and how to interpret the signals is the key.

There's also another side to the body's messages. Sometimes our ailments are the physical manifestations of emotional or spiritual problems. Disease and discomfort can be a signal to take action in the physical.

For example, a persistent cough may indicate that you literally need to "get something off your chest." A severe cold may be an indication that the body needs to take a rest, but just the recovery time from the cold may not be enough. When the body is well, dedicate some quiet time to see if you can discover the message of the illness.

A heart attack may be a message from the heart that it's not just the arteries that are hardened, but the attitude also. It could also be a message that you've allowed someone to "break your heart," and have kept your emotions locked within.

Back, shoulder, or leg pain may be a sign that you're trying to carry too large a load. In most of those cases, however, the load is only a problem because we have chosen to carry it. It's usually not even ours to carry. Pain in the lower back may signify an unwillingness to forgive. Resentment, hatred, and anger are burdens that weigh heavily on the physical body. True forgiveness is the way to lighten the load, but it's much more than saying we're sorry; it's forgetting and letting go.

While our employers, neighbors, and family members can sometimes legitimately be referred to as pains in the neck, it's our attitude towards them that may cause the discomfort to manifest its physical counterpart. The choice is up to us. We can grit our teeth and attempt to ignore those we consider a pain, we can separate ourselves from them, or we can accept them, love them, acknowledging that they are on a path different from our own and not subject to our control. But loving them does not necessarily mean loving their faults. We all have areas in need of improvement; we're all imperfect expressions of divine perfection.

One of the most powerful emotional and spiritual messages a body can send is the expression of cancer. Repressed anger, resentment, and feelings of unworthiness are all possible connections to this terrible disease. I've known people who have harbored extreme hatred for others for years, resentful when the other person achieves any sort of success. And I've seen those same anger-filled people suffer with the lingering and painful symptoms of this disease.

Sometimes an immediate cure is achieved when the sufferer acknowledges his anger and replaces it with unconditional forgiveness. Looking within is always a good first step towards recovery, for it is a well known fact that the body's functions, nerve impulses, and immune system are all affected by their emotional state. It's only logical that we can look to the state of mind of someone to determine their physical well being.

Our bodies are like good soldiers; they take orders and follow them without question. When we hold negative thoughts, we create an energy field that conveys a message to the body that brings about disease. Positive and uplifting thoughts send healing impulses. If we experience pain and disease, we need only to ask and listen to discover where we have strayed from our path.

Fear and worry stagnate the flow of energy within the body, and conversely, a calm, positive outlook opens the energy channels and creates the conditions that bring about good health. When we express fear, hatred or other negative emotions, we need only look to our bodies to see their physical manifestation. There we will discover the symptoms of our negative attitude, expressed as pain or illness. The body is the only vehicle through which we can reveal our suppressed emotions.

In those times when we are unable to discover the reason behind an illness, it is still best not to give energy to it. Continue to affirm good health and refrain from focusing upon your ailments for they will only be strengthened. Your body is the temple through which your spirit expresses in this world. Honor it. Listen to it. Treat it with love and respect, and you will be rewarded with the perfection that is Spirit.

Although the angels taught me many healing techniques, they stressed the importance of the state of mind of the person to be healed, and showed me why my efforts might not always result in healing. Today, when I ask my guides to explain how I should work with someone, they show me what is wrong and tell me what I am to say. When I tell the person what I've received, it's up to them to either accept or reject it. I'm only the translator. I don't try to force my interpretation onto another.

Many of those who have followed my suggestions, that is, the information I received from the angels, have been completely healed, and others have reported improvements in their conditions. However, I believe that each person is responsible for his/her healing. If we are guided to a healer, whether it be a medical professional or an alternative practitioner, it's up to us whether or not we choose healing.

This brings us to the issue of curing versus healing. Curing a disease, removing the symptoms, may only be temporary. Drugs, surgery, and other traditional forms of medicine are all focused upon curing.

Healing, however, comes from the Divine within, a condition that is permanent. It aligns the person with their true spiritual nature. While healing is sometimes influenced by others, it always comes from within. Spirit does not create illness; we do that on our own through our misuse of Divine Law. Healing then, is a reversal of that process, using the Law and the God within to restore perfect health.

Finally, our physical health is in direct proportion to our understanding and acceptance of our Oneness. If we see ourselves as one with our Creator, there can be no illness, for there are no limitations of any sort. Our acceptance of disease demonstrates a lack of faith and understanding.

Disease, however, should not be seen as failure. In fact, it can be the most wonderful of experiences. Our body's innate awareness of its divine nature may use disease as a means of redirecting our path, of helping us refocus. My personal experiences show me that this is true.

My new and joyous awareness of my true self was initiated through serious illness and my experience of death. I'm thankful for those events, even though at the time they were painful for both my body and emotions. Now, I try not to be so quick with those judgments. If I experience illness, I immediately go into my listening mode for I know that I'm either straying off course or have lost my focus.

Illness can be a great teacher. We need only to be good students, listening to the messages of our body with awareness that we are creatures on a mission to discover the self we have denied for lifetimes.

If we acknowledge our divine nature, it is no longer necessary to look to a future when a compassionate God may show mercy upon us. We will accept our heritage, our Oneness, expressed as perfect and healthy reflections of God consciousness.

CHAPTER 14

The Breath of Life

While it may seem strange, one of the most important healing lessons Maya taught me was learning how to breathe properly. She began by showing me how I'd neglected my body by continually starving it for air. But it's not just the oxygen that maintains good health, proper breathing teaches us how to pull in the energy of the universe to invigorate every cell of the body. Breath is the key to life; by learning a few simple techniques we can improve both our attitude and our health.

On more than one occasion I've been questioned by those who are skeptical of the benefits I describe. "If breath is so important, why hasn't my doctor told me about it?" they ask. "Aren't our bodies created with the knowledge of how to function?" And one woman insisted, "I'm alive. That shows I'm breathing. What else is there to know?"

Sure, we all breathe thousands of times each day. Our problem is that we have dramatically changed our lifestyle in the past century, and that change has altered the way we breathe. Most of our jobs require insufficient physical effort to force our bodies to properly utilize our lungs. Shallow breathing has weakened the muscles that help us breathe.

An important part of my healing work is to teach people how to breathe. My first workshop focused on the use of the breath, and those who come to me for healing, I first instruct in breathing techniques. I begin the healing process by having the person pull in several deep breaths.

Simply put, BREATH IS LIFE. Although we may survive for weeks without food and days without water, our bodies cannot survive more than a few minutes without breathing. But it's far more than pulling in small amounts of air into the lungs. Proper breathing sustains health. A daily ritual of breath exercises not only adds years to your life, it can add new dimensions to that life.

Proper breathing brings in oxygen to nourish our cells, but more importantly, allows us to pull in the powerful force that surrounds us. Called *Prana* in India and the Philippines, *Ki* or *Chi* in China, it has been recognized for centuries as being the source of strength and life. In Hebrew it's called *Ruah* and in Greek it's known as *Pneuma;* but whichever term you choose, most would agree upon its existence. My ancestors, the Cherokee, believed that a baby's soul was carried in on its first breath.

This force exists throughout the universe and is a source of immense power. While we often ignore it, this amazing energy surrounds us. It is in everything we see. Properly attuned, we can feel it and bring it into our bodies from trees, water, stones, and the earth. Because it exists in every molecule of air, we can recharge ourselves with each breath and store the energy in our bodies just as a battery stores electricity.

However, while our life may be sustained through shallow breathing, we can't reach our full potential if we fail to replenish our life-force through proper breathing. And our ability to help others is all but eliminated when we are not sufficiently filled with this force.

The following are several exercises designed to remove toxins, invigorate the lungs, stimulate the organs, improve one's overall health, and most importantly, fill us with the power of the Universe. The first shows how breath can be used to both energize and relax and releases the accumulated pain and stress caused by a busy lifestyle.

In the breathing exercises it is important to be aware of how the diaphragm assists the lungs. While many are not aware of its purpose or even its existence, the diaphragm is responsible for about two-third's of the respiratory process.

Located just above the stomach, it is the partition of muscles and tendons between the chest and abdominal cavities. A weakened diaphragm may be a symptom of lung disease, but many who consider themselves robust and healthy also suffer from limited lung function. If allowed to progress, such a condition leads to dependency upon the lungs and chest muscles for breathing, resulting in improper elimination of the lung's waste. By following a few simple exercises, one can restore lung function and bring health and vitality to the body.

Those with disease or lung-related conditions should consult their physician prior to attempting these exercises. While most of them will be done indoors in a seated position, back erect, feet firmly on floor, the Cleansing Breath should, as often as possible, be done outdoors, either standing or seated, facing the rising sun.

THE HEALING BREATH

This was the first breath technique I learned from Maya, and though it is simple, it is a powerful method for accessing your inner source of strength and wisdom. It can be done sitting or lying down, whichever is most comfortable.

A. Close the eyes. Take in a deep breath and release. Take in another and release.

Feel the body. Let your mind travel with your body. Let your breath guide you to areas that hold stress, tension, or energy.

B. Focus your breath upon one area of your body at a time. If you feel stress or pain, send your breath into that area. Form a picture of that area being healed; feel the stress releasing.

C. Concentrate upon another area of your body. Inhale and send the breath into that area. Feel the breath bring healing, relaxation, and calmness. Our minds control our emotions. We can heal the emotions with the breath, becoming more centered, more balanced, and filled with joy.

Let each in-breath bring in calmness and relaxation. As you release, feel the stress go out. The breath brings in energy. Energy and breath are life. Think of how few deep breaths you take each day. Make a commitment to change.

Begin each day by taking three deep breaths and slowly releasing them. Each night just before sleep take three more. Throughout the day when your energy feels low or you feel tension, use your breath to get you back on track. Most of all, be conscious of your breath and be in tune with it.

Over the years I've been guided to other breath techniques, each with a specific purpose. I have described several of them below:

THE CLEANSING BREATH

A. Inhale slowly and deeply through the nose. Pull air into the lungs until they are filled, then try to force in additional air until the lungs will hold no more.

B. Hold the breath for a few seconds.

C. With the lips only slightly parted, exhale through the mouth, forcing all of the air from the lungs. The escaping air will make a slight whistling sound as it is forced between the lips. When the lungs appear to be emptied, try to force out at least two more gulps of air.

D. Relax and hold the breath for a few seconds.

E. Repeat the above six to ten times.

Do this exercise every morning immediately upon rising and every evening prior to bedtime.

There are other breathing techniques that can be used both to improve overall health and to bring enlightenment to the mind. Those who need to strengthen the lungs muscles and capacity will find the following exercise helpful.

HOLDING THE BREATH

A. Inhale slowly through the nose, filling the lungs to capacity.
B. Hold the breath, retaining all the air in the lungs for a count of twenty.
C. Release the air slowly through the mouth.
D. Repeat, each time holding for a count of at least twenty.
E. Do ten breaths, more if possible, and do the exercise every day.

At the end of the first week, change the count in "D" to twenty-five, and each week thereafter add five more to the count until you can hold the breath for a count of sixty. This exercise greatly increases the capacity of the lungs and will enhance the body's energy. It is excellent for those whose diaphragm has become weakened through neglect.

The following exercise is great for giving yourself energy.

CELL STIMULATION BREATH

A. Slowly breathe in through the nose, tapping the chest area with the fingers as the air enters the lungs.
B. Place one palm on each lung area and hold the breath for a count of five.
C. Exhale through the mouth.
D. Repeat six times.

There is a rhythm to the cosmos, the movements of the planets, the changing of the seasons, the cycles of life, and the beating of our hearts. Everything is energy; everything is in motion; and everything has a rhythm that maintains its position in the universe. For centuries spiritual masters have known and understood the rhythms of life and have practiced rhythmic breathing, especially in conjunction with their meditations. The rhythmic breathing exercise helps bring you into harmony with your environment and with all of creation.

RHYTHMIC BREATHING

A. Inhale for a count of seven.

B. Hold the breath for a count of four.

C. Exhale slowly through the mouth for a count of seven.

D. Count four, then inhale once more.

E. Do at least fifteen breaths, but stop if the process becomes difficult.

As you become comfortable with the exercise, you may need to adjust the number of counts for your breaths and between breaths. If you pay attention to your body, you'll discover the rhythm that is right for you. As you continue you should be able to increase the counts, always being aware of how the rhythm feels. Over time you may notice your body swaying as your breathing adjusts to your inner rhythm and connects it with that of the universe. Some feel this exercise to be a great introduction to meditation.

Regardless of which breathing exercises you find helpful, it is important to follow one or more of them regularly in order to energize both your physical and etheric bodies. According to the angels, and confirmed by both science and medicine, proper breathing is much more than a simple autonomic process. I use a breath exercise each day to begin my meditation. I find that it brings me to a state of clarity that encourages Divine awareness.

Several years ago the angels guided me to produce what I call my "breath tape." In the tape I gave additional information on the "healing breath" described in the previous pages.

Whether you follow the techniques I describe or develop some of your own, I'm convinced of the importance of breath work. The impact it can have upon your life goes far beyond lung health, opening your awareness to its Divine potential and allowing the bounty of Spirit to flow as freely as a summer breeze. Breath can initiate an ever-changing journey of understanding, an exploration to the core of the self.

CHAPTER 15

Listening to the Heart

Our connection with our Creator

As the title of this chapter indicates we should listen to our hearts, but we are to listen in a way that is very different from what we might expect. Listening to your heart might more appropriately be described as listening with your heart.

Our hearts often know what our brains won't allow us to acknowledge, for our hearts don't rationalize, analyze, or criticize. The heart is aware of its connection with Spirit and understands its origins.

In many ways our hearts function much the same as our brains. Both organize information with the same types of nerves and cells, but the heart seems to add a previously unacknowledged dimension to the process. Traditional science and medicine have recently discovered many similarities between heart and brain function, and some of those more willing to risk their reputations have stated that the heart is superior to the brain in many ways.

As far back in time as we can discover written or pictorial records, humankind has been aware of the heart's special functions. Ancient civilizations recognized the heart as the seat of life, and their sacrifices to the gods showed how much importance they gave it. And though our minds often fail to acknowledge the heart's immense powers and abilities, our language vividly describes the dominion of heart. We speak of broken hearts, of talking heart to heart, giving heartfelt thanks, of people having good hearts, and of loving with all our heart. Cupid sends arrows into lover's hearts, the heart is the symbol for Valentine's day, and we may place our hands over our hearts as an indication of love, devotion, or commitment.

Science has now begun to tell us that there is a reason for such behavior, that the heart actually thinks, that its thoughts have a dramatic impact upon both the physical body and the environment in which that body resides. Some scientists and physicians now agree that the heart has a form of intelligence and may in many ways perform functions more advanced than the brain. The heart has a complex communication network that connects it to every cell, but more importantly, it may be our connection with the vast energy that surrounds us and forms our universe, our connection with Spirit.

If our heart is a powerful receiver and transmitter of energy, what helpful information can it tell us, and what may it tell others about ourselves? In order for us to reconnect with our heart energy, we must learn a few basic steps. As we learned in Chapter Ten, breath is where it begins. Practice the breathing routines and you will begin to experience the wisdom of your heart. Breathe deeply, be still, and listen. Don't concern yourself with thoughts that arise. Observe them and let them go. You may be bombarded with numerous random thoughts, but don't become discouraged. If you regularly practice your quiet time, you will make your heart connection.

As your breath takes you to a place of relaxation, visualize colors that are pleasing to you. See vibrant waves of color enveloping your body and transporting you to a place that is peaceful and safe. Color can help to clear your mind. Allow breath to bring color into those areas of your body where you feel tension or pain.

As you go into deeper states of relaxation, your brain may protest. Ignore its chattering. It may fight your attempts to remove it from external stimuli, filling itself with thoughts. You may recall grocery items you need, think about how you should respond to a boss or mate, worry about your financial situation, or any of hundreds of other useless topics. Don't let your brain pull you into that trap. Acknowledge the thoughts and send them away.

It's important that you not have an expectation from this process. Your purpose is not for any particular material or spiritual benefit; it's merely to listen and receive.

Some will call this meditation, and in a sense, they're correct. When we mention the word meditation to someone, however, their mind often paints a picture that is far removed from what I describe. What the angels taught me is that our heart can take us to a place where we realize our connection with all things—our Oneness with our God and with all of creation.

By practicing the breathing techniques and listening to our hearts, we will become aware of our true self; we will experience the enlightenment that is described in many of the ancient texts. It is through awareness of self that we are able to distinguish which path is our own. Such knowledge allows us to overcome the limitations of the body, a place where disease no longer has power, where negative thoughts cease to exist, and where we will truly be at peace with ourselves and our world.

How do we create this state amid the stress and confusion of our lives? We find it in the quiet, for it is only in the silence that we can hear God's answers to our questions and prayers. We also discover the need for patience. Enlightenment cannot be hurried. Learning patience has been one of my most difficult tasks, and it's a job far from complete. Early in my training I told Maya I felt I was ready for the next step. "Show me what's next," I said. I felt the pressures of time. Nearing forty, I felt I had to learn all she had to teach, and to learn it immediately. I was afraid I would have only a few years to share the wonderful lessons from the angels. I pressured her to accelerate the process.

"Be patient," she said. "There is much you need to know, and your haste will only make your journey more difficult."

I insisted. "I'm sure I'm ready." Her lessons had been amazing, but I wanted to see and learn more.

During that period a friend suggested I try a "sensory deprivation tank," a method intended to remove exterior sensory input so that the mind can reach an increased level of awareness and have contact with other dimensions and higher intelligences.

I jumped at the chance, eager to see if my expanded awareness would allow me to see some of the things Maya was withholding. Although I am somewhat claustrophobic, I was compelled to experiment with it. After all, if I could expand my awareness, the results would be positive. At the time that seemed a logical conclusion.

On the day of my appointment I awoke with reservations. I'd had a recurring dream where the word "patience" kept appearing on a blank screen. My curiosity eventually won out, and I drove to the place eager to see what I might learn.

Once there I sat in the parking lot for a few minutes, waiting for my appointed time. When I stepped out of my car and approached the door, I was stunned by a sign posted in the window. It read: "PATIENCE, THE PATH TO ETERNITY." The sign promoted an upcoming workshop, but I wondered if it was somehow intended for me. I paused for only a few seconds before entering, reminding myself it was only a simple sign. Yes, it was only a sign, but one I would later wish I had heeded. I stepped inside.

I was surprised by the way I felt upon entering, fearing the place might confirm the messages I'd ignored. Instead, it was bright and cheerful, and the aroma of fine incense filled the air. When I later analyzed the experience, I realized that I had made my choice, and my guides had ceased their coaching, allowing me to see what happens when I fail to listen.

I was led to the tank room. "You can change in here," the man said. When you are ready just get in and call me. I'll come and start it up."

As soon as I stepped inside, I went into a trance. I didn't even call the man back. I lost all sense of who or where I was. Horrible visions of death and destruction appeared to me. I was shown a vision of the future, but it was unbearable. I panicked and cried out for help.

The man in charge of the machine ran into the room. "What's wrong?" he asked.

"I can't do this any longer," I said. "I'm sorry, but I can't."

"You've only been in here for a couple of minutes. I haven't even turned it on. What happened?"

For me it had seemed like hours, and I wanted to get away. I couldn't describe my visions and didn't really understand what had happened. Every nerve ending in my body ached, raw from exposure to some terrible catastrophe. "I need to go," was all I could say.

I returned home, sickened by the pain and horror I had seen. What had possessed me to try such a stupid stunt?

I heard Maya's voice. "Now you understand why the information must come slowly. Your impatience has caused you pain. Do not fear what you can not understand. You will know those things when it is time. You have been shown a possible future. Don't be disturbed by such visions. Put away your fear. Perhaps now you will see that you are not ready for all I have to show you."

I wanted to forget what had happened, but the images were burned in my mind. "I'll never be ready for the things I saw."

"Yes, there will be a time, but it is not now. Your visions will serve to remind you that all cannot be understood on this plane. There is much I will show you when it is time to do so, and at that time you will understand and accept. Be patient and listen with your heart."

In the past couple of centuries we have spent a lot of effort trying to overcome those things that create problems for us. We've conquered enemies, battled with diseases such as polio and smallpox, studied methods of taming the weather, split the atom, worked towards the conquest of space, and now look to a future where man will be triumphant over all. In all of those battles we have lost our purpose, forgetting why we were put here in the first place.

We look at our world, our universe, as a hostile place that must be conquered before it destroys us all. We don't see ourselves as a part of that world, as having come out of it, but rather as pawns in a cosmic chess match who must be constantly alert in order to avoid destruction.

The opposite is true. Listening with our hearts allows us to reconnect with the world and lets us see how we are extensions of our wonderful planet. As the great American Indian, Chief Seattle, taught us, "All things are connected."

When we listen, we see through the illusion of ego. Because we are not separate from another, we can be neither better nor worse, above nor below any other person. Each person is equally a part of Spirit.

But just as ego distorts our vision of the world and our place in it, ego is a part of our world. Every thing and every thought is a part of the whole. Therefore, ego is not something to be destroyed, but is merely one more aspect of self. The secret is learning to keep things in perspective, and that's where the heart provides the greatest help.

Our heart shows us how there is nothing, yet everything, to be gained, how we can reach that state of awareness where we discover the true meaning of our lives and, most of all, what is real. We learn how to remain calm in the fiercest of storms, in those times our world seems out of control.

We'll not become instantly virtuous; on the contrary, we will appear much the same as before, locked within our human form with all its faults and frailties, and we will sometimes still experience emotions run wild. Our existence on this level depends on it. The difference will be in how we process our emotions, feelings, and thoughts. We will understand that we will never be able to overcome those who express evil or hatred; and we will see suffering as an equal to joy. Neither will have power over us.

Finally, when we've reached that state where we recognize everything as a part of the whole, our image of Spirit will cease to exist for we will understand that any image is limiting. We will lift the stone and Spirit will be there. We will gaze into the night sky and know that Spirit is there. We will see Spirit in our neighbor, our spouse, our enemy, and in our reflection in the mirror. We will see the connection—our connection—with everything in our experience. Then we will know God. We will see "I Am That I Am."

CHAPTER 16

Mind Pollution - A Spiral of Fear

What is it that keeps us from knowing the true self? What keeps us from connecting with our spiritual side, our Oneness? The angels told me I had contaminated my mind, creating a cloud that kept me from hearing my inner voice. I had focused my thoughts on useless bits of nonsense, leaving little room for the truly important things of life.

Maya once showed me how my brain was constantly receiving more information than my consciousness could handle and how blocking some of the input was critical to maintaining sanity. The brain must choose between thousands of pieces of information and select those it feels most appropriate to fulfill the mission you have selected. Those choices are made based upon an interpretation of our desires. The brain does not judge our choices; its sole task is to interpret and implement.

I often prided myself in being able to do more than one thing at a time, but my brain, accustomed to making me aware of those things I had shown it to be most critical, often overlooked messages from Spirit. It was preoccupied with the mundane aspects of my life, unaware of what was truly meaningful.

How do we change our focus so that our spiritual side comes first, so that our brain is aware of the importance of listening to the universe? It's simply a matter of commitment and practice.

Each day we're barraged with information from all sides, most of which is negative. Our evenings are often spent staring at TV screens—many feel impoverished if they don't have a television in every room—and our need for constant electronic input has caused a dramatic increase in the popularity of radio. We spend our commute and errand time listening to talk and news shows. The development of satellite radio now allows our favorite stations to follow us across the country. We read newspapers and magazines, surf the World Wide Web, all the while polluting our minds with negative and sometimes horrible stories, and we seem to think we need this input in order to enrich ourselves. The opposite is true.

It is vital to our very survival that we slow down the data so that we can receive the only information that is beneficial. A quiet time spent in the forest—no less than an hour—will open our minds to an incredible wisdom that comes both from Nature as well as our inner self.

How can we block out the noise in a society intent upon having its news broadcast continuously around the clock? How can we discover and learn to listen to our inner voice? There are several steps we can take.

The first is to change our habits and stop filling our minds with the negativity that pervades our society. Tune the radio to soothing music or listen to a CD. Even better, turn off the radio and try to reacquaint yourself with your inner voice. Avoid TV news altogether. Skip the first section of the newspaper. Make an effort to fill your mind with optimistic, inspiring thoughts. There is much that is encouraging; rediscover it.

Although we often complain about the lack of positive news stories, we are to blame. If we fail to buy newspapers or to watch TV, the editors and station managers will take notice. And when they realize that their focus on the negative is the problem, they will change. Whether or not we can muster sufficient numbers to create such change is unimportant, for we can control which radio and TV broadcasts come into our homes. Our power to choose can help us to create an environment that encourages spiritual growth.

We can also surround ourselves with those who share our beliefs and who support us on our path. If we are constantly in the presence of those with a negative outlook and whose focus is on the darker side of life, we absorb some of their energy. We will find ourselves agreeing with them and will have difficulty maintaining a positive outlook even when we are away from them. It's vital to both our health and our ability to focus upon our path that we avoid those who do not share our desire to maintain a positive outlook.

My angel guide's discussion of this issue provided me with insights that helped me understand how I might apply positive thinking into my life. "Thoughts are energy and create matter," they said. They showed me how focused attention to the negative events of each day gave energy to them and how pessimistic expectations of future events helped bring them into being.

Negativity is expressed through fear, worry, and guilt. If we fill our minds with such thoughts, we'll have no room for anything else. And the energy we send out will draw into our lives the very things we want to avoid.

Maya said I should make a daily habit of speaking optimistically about everything in my experience, and that I should avoid being pessimistic about anything. If I couldn't speak positively, I should keep quiet. She also showed me how unhealthy thoughts had contaminated my mind and constructed a barrier between me and Spirit.

"Do you know," she asked one day, "that your mind is sending out energy with every thought? When your thoughts are of fear or doubt you draw those people to you who will help you to transform those thoughts into reality. On the other hand, if you are filled with self-confidence, enthusiasm, hope, and gratitude, you will be a powerful magnet that will attract other positive and uplifting people—those who can help you achieve your dreams. You have the power and the choice is yours."

I learned how I had radiated failure and had encouraged thoughts of mistrust and fear in those around me. I saw how I had created my old job as "terminator," and I anguished over the negative way I had changed dozens of lives. But I also learned not to focus on my past mistakes. I couldn't change them. I was to begin a fresh start, avoiding such behavior in the future.

I knew I needed to dramatically change the way I viewed life, and I needed to overcome my fears. It would not be easy. When I look to my past, I wonder how I could have strayed so far from my path and become so fearful.

Fear, the demon that keeps us from reaching our goals, has entrenched itself in our society. We're afraid of the unknown, of change, and of what we may discover if we know our true selves. We suffer from "what if" thinking, imagining the worst possible outcomes in situations over which we have little or no control.

An old French proverb says:

Some of your griefs you have cured,
And the sharpest you still have survived.
But what torments of pain you endured
from evils that never arrived.

We sometimes paint bleak pictures from our expectations of how events will turn out, creating scenarios of disasters that never occur. Instead, if we will act in faith, knowing that the things that happen are in divine order, we can move ahead without the burden of our fears. Yes, things will happen that we won't like; some of them may even be painful for us. But if we refuse to act out of fear, we will become more receptive to the good that Spirit has to offer.

Is the pessimist correct in retreating into a cocoon of nothingness, trying to protect him or herself from the pain to come? Yes, the expected pain may come, but the question is: "Did the expectations, the doubts and fears, create the pain and draw it into being?"

Fear attracts those things of which we are fearful. Our negative expectations are powerful forces that often bring into being events that would never have occurred without our focused effort. It is a law of the universe that like attracts like. Our worries and fears are energy, drawing to us the very circumstances we wish to avoid.

We are all aware of how our eating habits, the proper intake of foods containing vitamins, minerals, and proteins, promote good health; and how consuming too little of the proper nutrients or too much sugar, refined foods, and other harmful substances creates illness. It is a logical step to assume that if our mind is constantly generating negative impulses, carried into every organ and cell by the marvelous circuits that lead from our brain, that negativity will be imprinted throughout the body. The energy of our thoughts, expressed in our bodies, will draw their physical counterparts to us with a force much greater than we might imagine. The action might be compared to the pull of a powerful magnet that allows it to lift a weight many times its own.

A proper mental diet is a prerequisite to spiritual growth. Ridding our minds of the fears that have constricted our development is a significant step towards attaining the life we seek. "As a man thinketh . . .," the saying goes, is as true today as when it was first written. Our thoughts—not only our conscious desires, but our worries, doubts, and fears—are powerful energies that dictate the condition of our lives.

We cannot change our environment without changing the thoughts we feed to our body. Thoughts are prayers to the Universe, constantly empowering those things we dwell upon, whether or not we consciously wish to manifest them. One of the true secrets to happiness, to reordering our lives, is learning how to control our thoughts, and the first step is to understand the way we give orders to our brains.

Changing my thoughts from those based in fear to ones that were positive and uplifting was one of the most crucial and important steps towards transforming my life and living in harmony with my spiritual nature. I had to teach myself how to choose my thoughts and how to reject those that did not align with the direction I knew I should follow. I had to learn how to control my emotions and how to protect myself from the negative influences from which

I was constantly bombarded. I was determined to succeed, and those who are willing to follow a few simple steps will be rewarded as I was. They will discover a new freedom, and the burdens that had weighed upon them for years will be removed.

Cultivating a good disposition is the final step, genuinely believing that our lives are holy, that we are indeed, children of God. "Begin each day with a brief prayer of thanksgiving," Maya said. "By doing so you affirm your connection with Spirit and with your higher self. You are telling the Universe that you acknowledge your Oneness, and you are confirming your intention to allow the fullness of Spirit to flow into your life."

In beginning the practice I started with a prayer in which I listed my many blessings. I found it helpful to compile a list of all the things for which I was thankful, and it turned out to be much longer than I would have ever guessed. Those who have difficulty with this task should take a careful look at the thoughts upon which they focus. We should easily be able to think of dozens of positive things for which we are thankful.

My morning prayer is not a grocery list of what I would like Spirit to bring into my life, rather it is my grateful acknowledgement for being given another day. I'm thankful for family and friends, those who have come into my life and with whom I have been privileged to work, for the physical comforts I enjoy, and for my health—regardless of any maladies from which I may suffer. I am grateful for the opportunities and lessons that come each day and for my awareness of my connection with Spirit and with all creation. My prayers pour out in a river of thanksgiving, for I am truly blessed that I can experience each new day and the wonders I know will come.

Developing a daily habit of giving thanks sets the tone for the day. We should smile as we pray, for smiles seem to reinforce our positive outlook and bring us closer to that time when our attitudes and our lives will be transformed. When the difficulties come—and some will come—we will only need to remind ourselves that each circumstance provides opportunities for growth; and for those we should also be thankful.

By connecting with our Creator each day we affirm our divinity and continue our agreement to allow Spirit to guide our lives. The practice will not instantly transform a life into one of eternal bliss, free of problems and pain, but it will make it easier to accept the difficulties when they come.

I recall a story I heard many years ago about a man who, while walking in the woods, had discovered the cocoon of a butterfly. Intrigued by his find, the man took the cocoon home and regularly checked to see if a butterfly might emerge. After a couple of days the man noticed a tiny hole in the cocoon, and he could detect the movements and struggle of the butterfly within.

The man watched for hours, fascinated by what appeared to be unfolding before him, but when progress seemed to have stopped, he attempted to offer help. He carefully enlarged the opening and watched as a butterfly slowly emerged. The butterfly's body, however, was grotesquely swollen and its wings small and shriveled.

The man waited patiently for the wings to expand and for the body to shrink to normal size, but that never happened. The butterfly remained in its disfigured state and died a couple of days later.

What the man in his impatience and ignorance had failed to understand was that the struggle of the butterfly to crawl out of the hole in its cocoon was Nature's way of forcing fluid out of the butterfly's body and into its wings. The man's efforts to speed up the process had resulted in failure and death.

Likewise, our struggles build strength and help us develop patience. While we may not appreciate those benefits when in the midst of a conflict, if we can separate ourselves from our pain and frustrations, we can begin the growth process. With heightened awareness we can soar above our old limitations on wings strengthened in the fires of adversity.

The transition into a state of awareness and connection with Spirit also requires patience. We must have faith with the understanding that our efforts will be rewarded in the proper time. When we are ready to take the next step, the pathway will open before us.

I needed to look for my answers in the silence, but first, I had to learn to be silent. It was there I discovered how to embrace my fears, how those fears had been born in my feeling of separation from God. Once I experienced my Oneness, my fears vanished.

I also had to learn how to acknowledge my mistakes and let them go. There were times I struggled with things from my past that I wished I could undo, but the angels showed me how I could use those mistakes to help me create a better future. I couldn't change the past, but I could change my behavior. My problems had taken years to create, and I knew I would need time to change my focus from negative to positive. Eliminating the pollution from my mind would remove the fear, anger, and resentment, and would keep me from drawing disease into my body. My challenge was to develop a state of mind that might help me create the life Maya had shown me to be possible. I knew I could do it. Once I had the tools, it was time to go to work.

CHAPTER 17

Discovering Your Lifeline

If we're on a boat and fall overboard, someone will toss us a life buoy and pull us to safety. If we suffer a heart attack, doctors and emergency medical personnel will perform CPR to try to restore us to health.

In the same manner there is a lifeline of enlightened friends and teachers to rescue us when we have strayed from our spiritual path. The key to finding those people is to listen, to be open to the sometimes subtle messages from Spirit. The adage, "When the student is ready, the teacher will appear" is not only true for finding a master or teacher, it can apply to great numbers of enlightened friends who are eager to assist in our search for our true self.

Once we set out on the spiritual path, it is important to look at those we have drawn into our lives. Are they positive, spiritually guided, and supportive? If not, they may significantly impede our progress. And, while I'm not suggesting you immediately sever your ties with those around you who seem unwilling to share in your journey, it's appropriate to consider how you spend time with them.

Remain faithful to your path, and surround yourself with those you trust to have your highest good at heart. Those who do not will drift away, uncomfortable in the higher energy of your developing spirituality and that of your enlightened friends. Love them and let them go.

How can you know for certain that someone shares in your spiritual goals and beliefs? You can always ask, and you can draw them into conversations where their goals and beliefs will become evident.

The best way, of course, is to ask Spirit, carefully listening for the answer. Spirit always responds to our requests, but be aware that the answer may come in an unusual or unorthodox manner—you may see a road-side billboard with an appropriate phrase, receive a message direct from your spirit guides, or the answer might come through your dreams. The possibilities are endless. Whatever the source, you'll always discover an answer if you pay attention.

When you begin to live a more spiritual life, that is, a life more in alignment with its divine path, you'll be guided to those who can help you. New and exciting doorways will open where you will encounter a world that is ready and eager to provide you with everything needed for your journey. You'll discover books, workshops, and study groups, the existence of which you may have been unaware.

I've often been fascinated by how such connections occur, and recall a time when I was struggling to improve, or more precisely acquire, a bit of patience. In the past I was a type "A" personality, especially during my corporate years. Even after my death experience I often struggled when understanding and awareness came slower than I wanted. I needed to move ahead. Once I had made the decision to change the direction of my life, I wanted it done immediately. I knew it was unrealistic to expect things to change overnight, but that didn't stop me from pushing. Developing more patience was the key to keeping me from continual frustration. I struggled with my lack of patience for months, aware that I needed help, guidance, or a catalyst that might propel me into a new and different perspective.

One day when I was out shopping, I stopped at a local card shop to buy some birthday cards. As I browsed the rows, I was startled by the sudden appearance of a middle-aged woman standing before me. She looked at me and smiled, and after returning her smile, I tried to re-focus on my purchases. The stranger's gaze seemed to hold me, however, and I stood there for several uncomfortable seconds trying to compose myself.

"Do you know what the gift of patience is?" the stranger asked.

I was flabbergasted and responded, "Why . . . uh . . . no. What is it?"

The woman produced a business card as if from thin air, offering it to me. I looked down at the card which read: "What is the gift of patience?" I stared at the words, wondering how the stranger could possibly know of my struggles.

I twisted the card over and noticed printing on the reverse. The word "PATIENCE" was printed in bold letters. I again read the front. "What is the gift of patience?" and then read the other side. The message was clear. I knew what I'd been missing.

Pushing for patience was no different from my efforts to achieve instant enlightenment. To achieve patience or anything else, I had to release the tension, to realize that there was no calendar showing when my search must be complete. When I live in the moment, there's always time for everything I need.

I looked up to question the woman about the card, how she had known what I had been puzzling over. She was gone! I hurried to the front of the store where a lone clerk was arranging a display on the cash counter. "Did you see which way that lady went?"

"Who? What lady?"

"The lady who was just over there." I pointed in the direction of where I'd been standing.

"Nobody's come in here since you did." the clerk responded. She raised her eyebrows and contorted her face. "You're the only customer I've had since lunch."

I ran out the door and looked up and down the sidewalk. My eyes scanned the parking lot. No one was in sight. I drove home without my cards.

I look back to that incident with a better understanding of why it happened. Was the woman real? Where had she come from? How did she know what I needed? I don't know, and it doesn't matter. She appeared when I needed help and provided the slight push I needed. And the card she gave me? I refer to it occasionally as a reminder of the sometimes simple ways Spirit responds to our needs.

A number of my friends have recounted similar experiences in discovering the help they needed. Some have had books literally tumble off the shelves and into their hands when those books held precisely what was necessary to help them along their path. Others have been led, through sometimes unusual circumstances, to workshops or teachers. And while your own experience may not be as dramatic, if you're open to Spirit, you may find your eyes drawn to a book, a magazine or newspaper article, or be provided with an opportunity to attend classes or lectures that are spiritually supportive.

The information we need is out there. When we make the commitment to follow our path, we find the exact pieces necessary and at the time they're needed.

The support group, the teachings, the friends, and teachers are there for us, and our guides will lead us to those we need. It's not a matter of finding the right teacher or searching for the right friends; it's a question of intention and desire.

If you are convinced that you absolutely must have a teacher or master to explain or assist you along your path, ask to be guided to one. If it's in your best interest, one will appear. But be wary of teachers who ask for money, especially large sums of money. While everyone on our wondrous planet needs certain tangible things for survival, and in our culture many of those things require money, there are lots of charlatans out there posing as masters who promise amazing results to those willing to pay their price.

In my experience true masters rarely seek us; instead, we are guided to them. And they will not boast of their accomplishments or abilities. Yet there are many who have been given an uncommon depth of spiritual awareness, and it's realistic to expect to pay them for their services. However, a careful evaluation will reveal those with limited knowledge and who are only willing to share it in order to gain wealth.

Be cautious. Listen to Spirit, to your guides, and you will find your truth. You will be led to those best suited to help you.

As I worked with my angel guides, I learned how to listen to my inner voice which I interpret to be Spirit speaking through me. Although I had been helped by my angels who had opened the doors to my true self, I learned that it was not necessary to have such experiences. We all have the ability to reach the God within. Why I had needed a death experience to awaken me, I didn't quite understand.

"Yes, there is no difficulty to opening yourself to Spirit," Maya told me. "But you had rejected Spirit's messages for years. Your fear blinded you, and your belief that there was substance in your material world had carried you far from your path. Each soul, each physical expression, is unique. Some are awakened by the words given to them; others by a healing touch. As your death allowed you to discover life, those who hear your story will share in the enlightenment you experienced.

"Do not question the process for you will only find frustration and disappointment in your search. Your path is yours alone. Follow it and do not concern yourself about the paths of others. There are many ways to Spirit. Those with a true desire to discover their path will find it in the appropriate hour."

My encounter with Maya had been no accident; she was drawn into my life by my inner calls for help. "I came because of your request," she once said. "Your true self knew the time was right for you to continue your journey, but your physical self would not give in so easily. It was time for your rebirth."

I had been unaware I was calling for help. I wasn't happy with the direction my life had been going, but I thought it was natural. Although I was happy to have found my new friends and teachers, I regularly wondered about the others who struggled as I had. Were they also calling for help? I wasn't sure.

During my work with Maya she explained how we have a dual awareness: the conscious, of which we are aware, and another part I call the superconscious, which maintains our connection with Spirit and with all of creation. It is often the conscious side of us that calls out for help—"Dear God, save me from this terrible disaster." Those sorts of pleadings rarely seem to be answered.

On the other hand, the superconscious is that part of us that is connected to Spirit and which is aware of both our path and how to best maintain our course. This superconscious might be thought of as the part that is Spirit or God.

Why, then, aren't we aware of the workings of this most important aspect of our being? When we consider the possibilities, the answer is clear. Our conscious mind cannot be fully aware of its "Godness." If it were, I believe, there would be no reason for our existence.

What would be the purpose for our lives if we were fully aware of the illusion? How could we participate in the mundane aspects of life if we knew we had the power to change at a moment's notice? We would be living a lie, unable to maintain interest in an existence that had no meaning.

We are here to have this physical expression, and to do so we must sometimes lose ourselves in the illusion. As long as it's not permanent, we're okay. When we join with our enlightened friends and teachers, we can have a glorious experience, and I don't want to miss a single minute of it.

CHAPTER 18

The Ways of Healing

While my initiation into the ways of healing was focused upon teaching me how to bring healing to others, I realized that many more would benefit if I could show them how to tap into the wondrous power that is available to us all. I was also reminded of my charge from the angels to both "teach and heal."

Frequently, those I encounter along the spiritual path are involved in some type of healing, and many have spent years studying various techniques or systems. While some are a part of the traditional medical community, the majority practice some form of alternative medicine.

Western medicine, however, does have much to offer. An emergency room doctor helped to bring me back, and I occasionally still need a physician's help. Their knowledge can also come from a divine source. My hope is that more of our doctors will become less rigid, willing to supplement their training with some of the ancient teachings and wisdom.

If I can awaken others to the true ways of healing, I have succeeded in my mission. Any healing I may bring is secondary. The key is in finding the pathway to understanding, for therein lies all knowledge. I share the lessons of the angels with those who are driven to learn about healing so that they may heal themselves and teach others.

The desire to heal is a powerful force that often causes us to seek to expand our understanding. One only has to open a metaphysical newspaper or magazine to find workshops and classes where the latest in alternative healing methods are taught. There are literally hundreds of healing modalities taught by thousands of practitioners around the globe, and many are divinely guided in their methods.

To become a healer is to understand and to heal ourselves. We can never have the kind of healing success we would like if we continually need healing for ourselves. It's not just important, it's critical to understand that point.

Many times the very ones who seek to learn about healing are those suffering from disease or illness, and it often seems that the spiritual path is accompanied by an onset of health problems. While that may seem unusual, a health crisis can be a great first step to exploring our relationship with the Divine within.

The next, and most important step is to begin to understand ourselves and our connection with our Creator and with all of creation. While we can certainly begin a study of healing, our understanding of both disease and health will come once our true self is exposed.

Where can we find our true self, and how will we recognize it once it is discovered? The angels taught me how to reach a state of meditation where I could understand my connection with my Creator and where my true self became evident. Such a practice, they said, was necessary to rid myself of the distractions of earthly life, and I now see what they meant. As I developed a routine of meditation and communion with my divine nature, I became more grounded in my spiritual side and less dependent upon the trivia that had once dominated my life.

My angel guides taught me the importance of breath work and how by observing my breath I could release my attachment to the physical world, peeling away the layers of illusion I had accumulated over a lifetime. Breath, I learned, holds the key to both health and enlightenment, providing the energy necessary for physical survival as well as spiritual growth. And conquering my breath proved to be one of the most difficult steps I would undertake.

As I described in the chapter, The Breath of Life, the simple act of breathing, while it may sustain our physical body, is not necessarily sufficient to properly energize the spiritual body. I learned that I needed to do much more than my normal shallow breathing, for out of such had been born both ill health and a life devoid of meaning. Once I had begun to master my breath and to understand my connection with my Creator, my heart was opened to learn the ways of healing.

When we see others suffering from physical or emotional disturbances, it's natural for us to want to help, but my teachers taught me the importance of understanding our role in the healing process. We are channels of Divine energy; of ourselves we have no power to heal and no power to discern who is to be healed. And healing does not come to everyone, they said. I had to learn to accept the fact that my efforts would not always achieve the outcome I desired.

When I asked Maya to explain, I was somewhat surprised by her answer. "If I was saved from death so that I might bring healing knowledge to others," I asked, "and if I follow your instructions, why will I sometimes fail?"

Her response was terse and to the point. "It is your obligation to use what you have learned to help others," she said. "Spirit, with agreement from the person to be healed, determines the best course for their healing to be expressed. Do not concern yourself with why or why not. Send your healing energies with Divine love and the proper result will always be achieved.

"The first step to healing," she said. "is to ask the person if they wish to be healed. While you may assume that they desire healing, and they may have indicated so in the past, have them speak the words. Have them confirm before you and before Spirit that they truly desire to be healed."

"Will those who tell me they wish to be healed receive a healing?" I asked.

"No, not as you may expect healing to occur. Remember, it is not your vision of what a person needs that is important; it is their destiny, their realization of their divine nature that must be achieved. Healing their physical body may be a part of that realization or it may not. There is also the issue of karma, as you call it, although your knowledge of that concept is much too limited. There are issues that deal with past lives, but the concept is far beyond what is possible for you to comprehend in this life. You should know that there will be many times when you will not understand the workings of Spirit, but you must have faith that Divine purpose is always being carried out."

I later understood that healing was not always the removal of a condition I perceived as illness. Sometimes my task was to provide comfort to the person or to their friends and family, to help them deal with the consequences of their disease. If I truly loved others, if I had compassion and a desire to help them, I had to put away my expectations and assist as I was divinely guided. I had to realize that while I might not observe a significant change in a person's condition, a healing may have occurred.

Learning that lesson was, and continues to be, a difficult process, for I want to understand. I need to know that I am doing everything possible and that the failure to heal is not my fault. I understand that I must trust Spirit, but sometimes I would like to have more information, more understanding of a situation in order to confirm my faith.

The key to healing is in asking Spirit for guidance and then listening for the answer. We must not let our expectations cloud our minds. If we are open, Spirit will show us what we must do.

I begin my healing sessions with a prayer for guidance and then I clear my mind, spending a few minutes listening for a response. It is important to be sensitive and to attune myself to the work at hand. When I am open, the correct answers always come.

Although Maya showed me how to use stones, crystals, and plants in healing, those lessons were more general in nature, that is, they were more for helping me understand how such objects can affect the human body and energy field. When I am to use such tools, I am always shown the specifics of what to use and how to use it. When I'm guided to use stones, for instance, I may be told to use one, two, or a dozen or more. While stones and crystals have an amazing capacity to assist us in our healing efforts, there are no specific techniques that work in every situation. Each healing is different, sometimes even with the same person. There are no healing rituals or tools that can be used in all situations. Ask Spirit, and follow the guidance you receive.

Finally, it is vital to understand the importance of proper cleansing. We must cleanse ourselves prior to and after a healing. Cleansing afterwards is especially important.

I have known healers who failed to properly cleanse themselves after a healing and who would later manifest the very symptoms they had removed from someone else. It's not unusual for healers to absorb such negative energy or disease, because we deliberately open ourselves and are generally more sensitive than the average person. Beginning with a prayer for protection is not always enough. As we lose ourselves in our healing work, our defenses sometimes fall, allowing the symptoms to enter our energy field and even our bodies. However, by following a few simple steps, we can avoid absorbing another's energy or disease.

A simple healing session might be as follows:

> **1.** Prior to beginning wash your hands and arms, either in a mild solution of salt water, alcohol, or witch hazel. This helps to remove any negative energy that might be passed to the person you are to heal.
> **2.** Open with a prayer for guidance. This is your opportunity to connect with the person being healed as well as to allow Spirit to show you how to proceed.
> **3.** Once you have received guidance as to what you are to do, visualize yourself surrounded by the white light of Spirit and ask to be protected.
> **4.** Proceed with the healing as guided.

5. If you have been directed to use your hands during the healing, visualize a bold fire burning before you and regularly flick your hands towards the fire to remove the negative energy that you are pulling from the person.
6. At the end of the healing session visualize yourself separated from the person with whom you've been working. It may be helpful to confirm the separation by making a motion of cutting the cord that has bound you to your patient. Such action helps you to detach from any negative energy that may have attached to you during the healing process.
7. Wash your hands and arms once more as in Step 1.

The above are just suggestions. Once you ask for Spirit's guidance, you may be directed to do other things. Listen with your heart and know that whatever you are guided to do will be in the best interest of the one you seek to heal.

CHAPTER 19

Gifts of the Spirit

Most of the people I've met during the past fifteen years have expressed a desire to make a difference in the world. They want to believe that their life has meaning, that they have made a worthwhile contribution. What they want, I believe, is to create the kind of profound change that we have seen from great spiritual teachers and leaders such as Gandhi or one of the present day gurus we see on TV. And some of them will do just that.

Every life makes a difference. Each one is worthwhile, even though we may not see the results or understand its purpose. We don't need to focus upon being recognized by our peers as great leaders or teachers. The most important thing we can do is to be ourselves, the person we chose to be in this lifetime. And that, sometimes, may be to lead a life that is hardly noticed. It's not for others to decide what our contribution has been or should be. Only we can know that. Knowledge of our purpose comes when we listen to Spirit.

The key is listening without judgment. We usually have an idea of the direction we would like our life to take, but such ideas often come from ego or desire, and may have no relationship with our true purpose. We should be flexible and willing to take that great leap of faith to follow the guidance we receive from Spirit. I know of no other way.

In my case I would have never selected the path of healer or teacher. Though my old life brought me little joy or satisfaction, I had no idea it needed to change, unaware of the possibilities before me. It took a death experience to get my attention. Fortunately, it doesn't have to be that difficult. I was blinded to my path and had never experienced the true self. All that had been necessary was a willingness to listen. Of course, I first had to acknowledge that their might be another path for me.

I encourage everyone to ask for guidance. That is the first step. The second is to listen for the answers. They may not come as we expect, but if we are aware of our surroundings we will receive a response. I've had them come from friends, heard them on my radio, and even seen them printed on highway billboards, When we are ready for our answers, and when we listen, the answers always come.

One example of how Spirit guided me in a direction I would have never considered is what I call my "creations." Several years after my death experience I asked Spirit for a gift, a creative way for me to express some of the wonderful healing energies I had received. I thought it might be nice to work with clay or to paint pictures that would be inspired and filled with the power of Spirit. A few weeks later Maya told me a gift was coming.

I was excited. Eager to begin my painting or pottery, I awaited directions on how I would begin. Would a teacher appear or would I just be divinely inspired and begin my artistry without physical help? I waited for the answer. While I waited I checked out stores that carried the art supplies I was sure I would soon need.

I had not mentioned my request to anyone and was surprised when a close friend stopped by one day. "I have something for you," she said. She reached into a bag and pulled out a large spool of yarn. "I don't know why I bought this, but I felt I should bring it to you."

"I don't know either, but thanks . . . I guess. It's pretty."

My friend told me she had been browsing through a store when she found herself in the crafts department. "You know I'm not one to do crafts. Heck, I can hardly sew on buttons, but I felt drawn to the crochet section. This spool of yarn seemed so perfect. Something told me to buy it for you. I hope it makes sense to you, because it didn't to me."

I thanked her, but after she had left, I stuck the yarn in the closet. I had no idea what to do with it. I knew nothing about crocheting and had no interest in learning.

I had forgotten about the incident until one day a couple of weeks later. I was relaxing with my morning coffee and reached to put my cup on the table next to my chair. There beside me was a bright pink crochet hook. I had no idea how it got there. It certainly wasn't mine for I had never tried or even considered taking up the hobby.

I was so puzzled I called Mike at work and asked if he had bought it. I thought he might have seen the yarn in my closet.

"What's a crochet hook?" he asked. "I don't know what you're talking about."

I returned to my chair, more perplexed than ever. "Is this some kind of cosmic joke?" I asked aloud. I wasn't interested in crocheting—or so I thought.

I put the hook in the closet with the yarn, thinking I might give them to someone who was interested. Their appearance was strange, but I gave them little attention until something even more bizarre happened a few weeks later.

Again I was having my morning coffee, when I looked down to my lap. There was the spool of yarn and the hook! I jumped up and ran to the closet. The shelf was empty.

When I returned to my chair I picked up the yarn and pulled out a short section, then began working it with the hook. I had no idea what I was doing. I didn't know a single crocheting technique.

The yarn slid smoothly through my fingers as I worked it back and forth. I watched my hands, fascinated by what they were doing. It was as if they didn't belong to me. Their movements were precise and guided and they seemed to know exactly what to do. Soon I was holding a small square. I lifted it up and stared at it for several minutes. It looked perfect. Although I didn't know if I had done it correctly, the piece seemed consistent with others I had seen in the past. I put it on the table and laughed, wondering about what had happened.

The next morning, as soon as I was seated, my hands immediately reached for the yarn, and I began crocheting. I worked for more than an hour and the piece began to grow. I looked at it and tried to guess what it could be used for. Nothing came to mind.

A few weeks of crocheting passed before I discovered what I was making. One morning as I picked up the yarn, the angels had me connect it in a few strategic places. My work had begun to take form. The piece would later become a magnificent jacket. The angels called it "*Navaho Woman*," and it was an incredibly beautiful design. I can say that because it wasn't my creation; it had come from the angels.

That first piece, perhaps because of how it came into being, was my favorite, and I cherished it for several years. I had received some subtle nudges from my guides to give it to a friend, but my stubborn side refused to comply. The jacket was special and I didn't want to part with it. I hid it in the back corner of my closet, thinking they might forget. They didn't.

I sometimes wonder if the guides laugh when I fail to see through the illusion, when I cling to things as if they are real. My desire to keep *Navaho Woman* was one of those times. As usual, the guides didn't give in.

One day a workman came to make a repair and had to access one part of my closet. When he was finished I went into the room where he had been working and found my favorite creation lying on the bed. "You're supposed to gift me," it seemed to say. It was the only thing the workman had removed, a reminder to give it to my friend. I reluctantly agreed, and invited the friend over for coffee.

I'm sure it's hard to understand my motivation, but I had seen the jacket as my gift, something tangible from Spirit. In one last effort to be sure the guides wanted me to give it away, I devised a plan I thought fair. I would put the piece out, and if my friend didn't mention it, I would interpret that to mean I should keep it. Even after all my experiences, I sometimes still miss the big picture.

Of course I did eventually get the message, and I began to understand what the creations were about. They were more of the healing tools I had been given. I gave *Navaho Woman* to my friend, and did it willingly, knowing that keeping it wasn't where the meaning was. The significance was being allowed to create them for others. That was my gift. When I finally understood the purpose of the pieces, sharing them was easy. It was a great honor for me to have been chosen to make them. I'm grateful for the opportunity, and feel somewhat embarrassed for my earlier lack of eagerness to let others experience their healing energies.

Now when I'm guided to pick up the yarn, I enjoy the process, wondering who will be the recipient. At the time they're being made, I usually have no idea. Some of the creations have hung in my closet for months before someone would come by and I would immediately know a piece was for them.

It's as if the yarn is infused with healing energy, and I suppose it is. Recipients have told me of being healed from chronic illnesses after wearing one of the creations for only a short time. Others have spoken of an uplifting, almost euphoric, effect; and some have felt their connection with Spirit to have strengthened as soon as they donned their piece.

Even though I never learned how to paint or sculpt, I treasure what I received. I experienced the gift of love, of being able to pass on something meaningful to others. The pieces I've made, as well as those that may come in the future, allow me to connect with others in a way that might not have been possible through any other means. I'm grateful that Spirit has allowed me to share a small bit of the joy and peace that has come into my life.

There are gifts for each of us, but we often don't see them because we fail to pay attention. We blind ourselves to the obvious and turn away from things we feel are incompatible with our goals or lifestyle. Listening to the subtle urgings of Spirit can open us to new and wonderful ways to express and share the bounty of our universe. It's taking that first uncertain step that creates so much doubt.

There are countless opportunities for us to express our divine nature just waiting to be acknowledged. It is our job to discover them. Seek guidance and ask for clarification when you don't understand. Ask. Then listen, and don't prejudge the answers that come.

You may be an attorney and be guided to paint, a physician guided to lead a scout troop, a carpenter guided to study herbal medicines, or any of a million other possibilities. The point is that we must not ignore the guidance we receive, regardless of how bizarre it appears on the surface. There are multiple gifts for each of us, ways we can share our talents and our inner resources which come from Spirit. The choices are ours. We can pretend we are captains of our destiny, on a solo voyage through life, or see ourselves as victims, puppets awaiting the tug of the master's string. Either way we overlook our Divine Self, our connection with our Creator.

We are neither alone nor subordinates, but are co-creators in the worlds of our experience. We decide whether to make our lives ecstatic or miserable or somewhere in between. And hiding behind the veil of indecision doesn't protect us, for that too is a choice.

CHAPTER 20

The Future

What did I learn from the angels that would help me to deal with an uncertain future? How can their lessons save us from the pain that fills our world? Will their guidance show us how to avoid the suffering and confusion of our chaotic existence?

The angels taught me how to discover the purpose of my life, my Divine connection, and how to listen to my inner guides. They showed me what I could say to others that would unlock the doors of a mind ready for awakening, and finally, how to keep the events of life in perspective, helping me avoid the pain I sometimes created for myself. In my years of learning from them I also learned the meaning of love, how to share it with friends and family, and how I could send it out to those in my community, as well as, and most importantly, to all the world.

My time with the angels changed the direction of my life and the way I view my experiences. I learned how to ask for guidance and how to recognize and understand it when it comes. I was taught healing techniques that allowed me to meet and help many wonderful people. Through all the struggles of my life, and continuing through the wondrous and often unexpected events into which I'm guided each day, my faith in the ultimate goodness of humankind has grown incredibly stronger. Though I see and hear of horrible and destructive events occurring around the globe, natural disasters of horrendous proportions, war and hatred between peoples, and the outbreaks of terrible diseases, I know we are being guided towards a reunion with our Creator. We are on a divine path of discovery, to become aware of our relationship with each other and with Spirit. Of that I'm certain.

How can we prepare for our enlightenment? How are we to react to a neighbor who threatens violence? How can we allow the pain and suffering to continue? We can do it with lots of love and understanding and an intense desire to awaken to our true self.

Through my work with the angels I've learned important steps that can reduce our level of frustration, help us to recognize our path, and guide us to inner peace. The most important is to understand the meaning of love. Once we see ourselves as beings of love, coming out of a Divine Source that is pure love, we begin to see our connection with everything else in our experience. When we understand how we are all segments of one great body, we can do no harm to another, for to do so is to harm ourselves. As Chief Seattle said: "Man did not weave the web of life; he is merely a strand in it. Whatever he does to the web, he does to himself."

How can we be filled with hatred for another when we recognize the other person to be one limb on a body of which we also are a part? How can we fail to love all of creation if everything comes from Divine Source? When we recognize and honor the Source in all, hatred and prejudice cannot exist, and love becomes our guiding principle. When we expect the best from everyone, knowing that all is in Divine order—even though we may not understand what is occurring—our expectations will be met. The laws of the Universe never fail.

As we become enlightened, we see how many of our problems come from ego, the misguided understanding that we are separate from everything else. That belief can only be maintained when we ignore our relationship with Spirit. I don't see us as separate, disconnected, and unequal forms that have merely evolved to our present state. We are equal instruments in a Divine symphony, each performing our individual tasks, but each necessary to complete the whole. Just as a musician may sometimes fail to understand the purpose of the conductor's actions—why one instrument seems to be favored over another—we are sometimes unaware of the big picture. What we may not see is how our conductor uses each of us to produce a wondrous melody, a work much more glorious than the brilliance of one part.

Our failure to acknowledge the good in others is really a failure to see God in them. And when we fail to see God in others, we cannot recognize God in ourselves. Our ability to love is directly related to our awareness of our divine nature and that of our neighbors. When we express hatred, it comes back to us; but when we express love, we receive the same in return. The great teachers throughout time have all known this.

The next step in our discovery is to learn how to listen to our inner guides, the voice of God within. Though teachers and books may help us understand where our path lies, they aren't required. We can discover our path on our own. To do that we must listen to our inner voice. It will show us where we need to go. Listening makes us aware of the great power within and helps us grow in both understanding and wisdom. The centuries have produced sages who all pointed to the same source of knowledge and wisdom. That source is within each of us in equal measure. Teachers are like therapists. Their job is to help us discover our true self. The key is to quiet ourselves and to look within. The answers are already there.

In my work with others I'm sometimes asked about trusting our inner guides, how we can be sure that the voice is true. The answer is simple. If our intention is to know ourselves, to know the Spirit within, and if we ask for guidance and then listen for answers, we will receive the information that is right for us at that time. Spirit does not mislead us. If we are sincere and listen, we will discover the answers we need. Truth will come; we will know it; and it will certainly set us free.

Finally, many times I've been approached by those who are in constant turmoil and who are struggling to find peace, those whose lives seem surrounded by pain and suffering. When they ask for help, I tell them of the prayer of St. Francis, a prayer that reminds us of our purpose.

Lord, make me an instrument of Your Peace.
Where there is hatred, let me sow love;
Where there is injury; pardon;
Where there is doubt, faith;
Where there is despair, hope;
Where there is darkness, light;
And where there is sadness, joy.

Divine Master, grant that I may not so much seek to be consoled, as to console;
To be understood, as to understand;
To be loved, as to love.

For it is in giving that we receive;
it is in pardoning that we are pardoned;
And it is in dying (to self) that we are born to eternal life.

The prayer says it with Divine simplicity. In order to have peace in our lives, we must bring it to others. Searching for personal gratification is succumbing to ego and shows that we believe ourselves to be separate from all else. When we see our Oneness, accept our place in Ultimate Reality, we have no need to try to bring anything into our lives, for we already have everything that is possible. What more could we ask?

Epilogue

More than once while working on this book I found myself struggling with how to convey Myra's feelings and emotions. Doing so with accuracy was one of the most difficult tasks I've ever undertaken. There were times I wanted to stop, wondering if I might never complete it. I spent hours on the phone and meeting with her in person seeking clarification of events she had described or quizzing her about the specifics of something she had said. I didn't want my feelings or ideas to cloud what I considered an important work.

There were also times I struggled with my own problems, and I sometimes found myself mentally calling for her help. When I would take time to stop and listen, as she so often suggested, I would feel her warm hand on my shoulder or hear her comforting voice. On at least two occasions I smelled the distinctive aroma of her pipe tobacco as if she were there with me. Sometimes when returning to my work, I would open the manuscript to a passage that would be painfully appropriate for whatever dilemma I had faced. It happened so often that I almost began to expect it.

But I also remember how Myra had stressed the importance of looking for our answers within and not being dependent upon others. At those times I would remind myself that the solutions to my problems are always within my grasp. If I listen, I'll find them. I'm also aware of the great honor of having been chosen to help write this book. Though it has been difficult at times, it has truly been a labor of love. I recall what the angels told Myra when she had questioned doing the TV special: "If one person is helped, would it not be worth it?"

Yes, it has been worth it and much more. Reaching one person can change the world, for they can awaken others who can tell others, who can tell others . . .

Myra Starr is one of the most incredible individuals I've ever known. She is connected with the world of Spirit in ways most of us cannot imagine. Working with her I have come to understand that she was not the only person touched by her death experience. Her angel guides influenced me in ways I can't begin to describe, and their healing message will reach thousands more as it spreads across the globe.

John Mulkey

Made in the USA
Columbia, SC
17 June 2022